HOW TO GIVE YOUR KIDS $1 MILLION EACH!

HOW TO GIVE YOUR KIDS $1 MILLION EACH!

...and it won't cost you a cent...

Ashley Ormond

Wrightbooks

This edition first published 2011 by Wrightbooks
42 McDougall Street, Milton Qld 4064

Office also in Melbourne

First edition published in 2006 by Wrightbooks

Typeset in ITC Giovanni 10.5/14pt

© Ashley Ormond 2011

The moral rights of the author have been asserted

National Library of Australia Cataloguing-in-Publication data:

Author:	Ormond, Ashley.
Title:	How to give your kids $1 million each! – and it won't cost you a cent / Ashley Ormond.
Edition:	Australian bestseller now updated
ISBN:	9780730375487 (pbk.)
Notes:	Includes index.
Previous ed.:	2006.
Subjects:	Saving and investment. Savings accounts. Children — Finance, Personal.
Dewey Number:	332.6

Cover design by Brad Maxwell

Cover image: © iStock International Inc./Vaide Seskauskiene

Microsoft Excel graphs reprinted by permission of Microsoft Corporation

Printed in Australia by Ligare Book Printer

10 9 8 7 6 5 4 3 2 1

Disclaimer

Contents

Acknowledgements

I am indebted to the many people whose questions over several years inspired me to write the first edition of this book, and to the many thousands of readers who provided a wealth of valuable feedback and suggestions. Special thanks also go to Anne-Marie Esler from Centric Wealth for her assistance on updating the complex rules on taxation for children. This book would not have been possible without the tireless efforts of the team at John Wiley & Sons, and without the patience of my family.

Disclaimer

This book is intended to provide general information only, to assist readers to make their own decisions and choices. It should not be construed as a recommendation or a statement of opinion about any financial products. It is not intended to influence a person or persons in making a decision in relation to a particular financial product or class of financial products, or an interest in a particular financial product or class of financial products. This book is intended for educational and instructional purposes only.

The information in this book has been prepared without taking account of readers' individual objectives, financial situation or needs. Because of this, readers should, before acting on the information, consider the appropriateness of the information, having regard to the reader's objectives, financial situation and needs. If the information relates to the acquisition, or possible acquisition, of a particular financial product, readers should obtain a product disclosure statement relating to the product and consider the statement before making any decision about whether to acquire the product. Readers should obtain individual financial advice from a licensed investment adviser, and legal and tax advisers to determine whether information contained in this book is appropriate to their needs.

This book is not intended to constitute personal financial advice. It merely describes what has worked for the author. Where particular products or companies are mentioned, it is done so because they have been found by the author to be useful and/or they are used as examples of what may be available in the market.

The author declares that from time to time he may hold interests in securities and companies mentioned in this book. In fact, several of these are used as actual examples in the book. Other than as an investor, neither the author nor any related or associated entity receives any financial benefit or other benefit from the inclusion or mention of any of the securities, companies or products mentioned in this book. Other than as an investor, the author has no association or relationship whatsoever with the providers or issuers of any financial products or companies mentioned in this book. The author will receive royalties from the sale of this book. No company or product provider or issuer, whether mentioned in this book or not, contributed in any way to the costs associated in writing the book, or provides any financial or nonfinancial benefits to the author or any parties related or associated with the author.

About the author

Ashley Ormond has been in the finance game for 25 years, including several senior executive roles in major international banking and finance groups. He has been a director of several companies including listed, private, charitable and not-for-profit organisations. He has degrees in economic history, law and finance, has lectured on capital markets for the Securities Institute of Australia (now FINSIA), for CFA Institute courses, and is a CFA® charter-holder. He has written three books on finance and investing, and is a regular media commentator and conference speaker on financial topics.

Ashley is the owner and director of Investing 101 Pty Ltd, which holds an Australian Financial Services License (AFSL 301808). He is also a director of Third Link Investment Managers Pty Ltd (AFSL 321611), from which he receives no fees or other benefits, and which donates all management fees (net of expenses) to the charitable sector.

Ashley is not involved in selling courses, trading systems, seminars or any other type of get-rich-quick scheme. He receives no commissions or benefits from any product provider mentioned in this book. He simply wrote this book to provide information on building long-term wealth for ordinary Australians, many of whom can't afford the services of financial planners or other professionals.

Ashley and his wife semi-retired in their early 40s and are bringing up two young children in Sydney, who are also building investment funds of their own by following the plan outlined in this book.

Preface

This book is unlike most personal finance books you may have read or seen. It doesn't contain promises to reveal the 'seven secrets of success', the 'nine magic keys to wealth', the '10 things wealthy people know that you don't', or anything so dramatic. There are no such things in real life. Nor does this book require you to attend any seminars or courses, or buy trading systems. The plan I have developed is not a get-rich-quick scheme. It takes many years of patient investing to build real wealth.

Every day we are bombarded with advertisements for different types of investments — on television and radio, in newspapers and magazines, on the sides of buses, and via spam emails and even internet pop-ups — all promising wealth and happiness. Almost every day, new financial products are launched in an already overcrowded market, and it seems that they are getting more and more complex, using all sorts of fancy structures, financial wizardry and layers of fees. Many of these products are so complex that even professional investors need teams of accountants, lawyers and tax experts to understand them.

But there are a number of relatively simple, low-cost, tax-effective, low-maintenance products that are available to virtually everybody who wants to build long-term wealth. Even small investors can start out with as little as $1. Many of these products have been around for 50 years or more and continue to work for investors year after year, decade after decade. But finding them among the thousands of other products is a bit like trying to find a needle in a haystack.

This book doesn't contain any brilliant new ideas that you can't find anywhere else. The plan I outline is the result of lessons I have learned from over 25 years of investing and working in the finance game. What I have tried to do is to set out some practical steps and processes that just about anybody can put into place to build long-term wealth, as long as they stick with it. The book is designed to help people overcome some of the hurdles that they may come across every day, set goals, avoid scams and reach the goal of giving their kids $1 million each.

Since the first edition of this book in 2006 there have been some dramatic changes in the financial landscape. The global financial crisis of 2008–09 saw the collapse of many scams and unsustainable products. This is unfortunate for the investors who were caught up in them, but it is a reminder that the basic principles of investing are still valid and that it is possible to build wealth with relatively simple approaches that make sense in the long run.

See a licensed financial planner, if you can

Legally I am obliged to advise readers to see a licensed financial planner before purchasing any financial products, but this may not be much help for the many ordinary Australians who can't afford one.

Most financial planners will only take on new clients if they already have at least $100000 or so to invest. The financial planning industry is geared to deal with clients with a lump sum to invest — from retrenchment, retirement, the sale of a business or an inheritance. For people who do have a lump sum to invest, receiving advice from a licensed financial planner is a necessity. However, many ordinary Australians starting out with small amounts will simply not be able to afford one. But all is not lost for ordinary Australians who want to build wealth and financial security. There are some very simple investments available that are often just as effective as, and much cheaper than, the expensive managed funds sold through financial planners. Building long-term wealth need not be out of the reach of ordinary Australians. This book will show you how you can do it.

Ashley Ormond
Sydney, January 2011
<ashley@investing101.com.au>

Part 1

ON YOUR
MARKS

Chapter 1

Giving your kids $1 million each

1.1 The plan

I began developing this plan in 1994, when my daughter was born. Now I'm also following it with my son, who was born six years later. They are now 16 and 10 years old, and we are on track to be able to give them $1 million each under the plan. It's pretty simple and just about anybody can do it — starting with as little as $1. And it won't cost you a cent. You can give them much more than $1 million — you can also give them the knowledge and skills to keep it, manage it and make it grow.

Right now you're probably saying to yourself, 'That's impossible. This guy's crazy.' Or, 'It sounds too good to be true — it will never work!' This is a natural reaction and it's good that you're sceptical. But I guarantee that if you spend a couple of hours reading about how the plan works, you will agree that it makes sense and will be keen to get started. In fact, you will probably say something like, 'I wish I had started doing this years ago!'

Without doubt the single most common comment from readers of the first edition of this book and my other books has been, 'why didn't somebody tell me about this years ago?'. The good news is that it's not too late for you to secure your financial future, and it's certainly not too late for your kids.

So what is the plan? First of all, putting aside the problem of actually coming up with the $1 million for a moment, let's dream about that $1 million we are going to give our kids. Wouldn't it be great to be able to give them a financial foundation for life so they never have to worry about money? Wouldn't it be great if they didn't have to live by surviving from payday to payday like most people? To not have to worry about credit card debts or car loans or mortgages? To be able to choose their careers based on what they loved doing, rather than what paid the most, or what marks they get at school? To be able to take time off to travel, start a business, or work for a charity — if that's what they wanted to do? To be able to retire when and where they wanted? This financial freedom would be a fantastic gift to give our kids.

I also thought about some of the potential problems with the plan. Even if we are in a position to give them the money, how do we stop them from spending it all as soon as they get it? We have all heard stories of how lottery winners just frittered their windfall away in a few short months and ended up with nothing. How do we get them to appreciate the value of money? How do we ensure that they know how to manage money and know how to make it grow? How do we help them avoid being ripped off by all the so-called experts who can't wait to get their hands on the money? How do we help them to steer clear of dodgy investment schemes?

So, with all these things in mind I created a plan that would give the kids $1 million each but that has some rules in place so they don't immediately spend it. The plan gets them involved in managing the money and making it grow, so they will continue to make it grow after they get their hands on it. It also gives them the skills and knowledge to deal with so-called experts like accountants, lawyers, financial planners, brokers and insurance salespeople, and helps them avoid being ripped off by dodgy investment schemes.

The aim of this book is to show how almost any parent can start the plan, stick to it and invest well to build long-term wealth for their kids. But how do we come up with the $1 million? Well, this is actually the easiest part of the whole plan. It's very simple. For each child, if we simply put aside $1 every day, starting from the day the child is born, invest it in growth assets, reinvest all the earnings and never spend it, they can end up with $1 million by the time they are 50 years old.

If 50 years is too long to wait, we can put in $2 per day, which would get to the $1 million mark five years sooner, when the child is 45. However, if we were to begin by putting in $2 per day and increased the contributions by 5 per cent each year, that would cut another five years off the plan. If we wanted to get really serious, we could start by putting in $5 per day and increase the contributions by 5 per cent each year — this would reach $1 million in only 32 years. One reader even wrote that they had started a 25-year plan for the $1 million target — they kicked off the fund with $1000 from the government's 'baby bonus', set their contributions at $300 per month (they gave up smoking, which was costing them $10 per day or $300 per month!), set the contributions to increase by 7 per cent each year, and chipped in $1000 each year as the child's birthday present. This plan works with any amount of money. The more we can put in, the sooner we get to $1 million. But I will use the basic $1 per day plan for the examples in this book because most families can probably afford to put away $1 per day. In chapter 2 I look at some of the ways to find that $1 per day.

Keep in mind also that the aim of this plan is not to give the kids a big bucket of cash now so they become spoilt brats. They should go to school, get a job, build their careers or businesses, and do all the things we did — and more. But we also want them to have enough money behind them to enable them to have more control over their lives.

The aim of the $1 million is not so our kids don't ever have to work. Just about everybody needs to work to contribute to society, to meet challenges and grow from them, to meet friends, and to give them something to complain about at the pub on Friday nights! The aim of the $1 million is to enable them to do what they really want to do with their lives, rather than what they have to do just to make ends meet, which is how most people get by.

But what about the part that says it won't cost us a cent? We, the parents, will be making the $1 per day contributions for the first 10 to 15 years of the plan. That's when the kids can start to take over and contribute $1 per day — from their pocket money or money from part-time jobs. As they grow up they will learn more about the plan and will get into the habit of putting their own money away for their investment fund.

We will only be contributing around $7500 over the first 15 years, and this money is a loan, not a gift. That loan is to be repaid when the kids are, say, 30 or 40 years old — it's up to us to set the rules. By the time they reach 30 the $1 per day fund will have grown to around $110 000, and by the time they reach 40 it will have grown to around $330 000. So they can repay the loan of $7500 and it will only put a tiny dent in their fund, allowing them to continue on the path to $1 million.

That's it! The plan is simply based on the principle of compounding. There have been dozens of books written about the 'miracle' of compounding and how money can grow over time. But it's not a miracle at all — it's just simple maths. The contributions to the plan start at $372 in the first year ($31 per month) and add up to a total of $53 000 over the full 50 years (including the parents' contributions in the early years, plus the child's contributions after they take over the plan). But, because all investment earnings are reinvested in the fund, the contributions plus all the reinvested investment earnings turn into $1 million! That's the so-called miracle of compounding. I will cover compounding in more detail in chapter 4, where you and your kids will be able to do the maths and check the numbers yourselves. We also cover fees and taxes, which turn out to be very favourable for our $1 per day investment plan.

To reach $1 million by investing $1 per day when your child is born requires that the investments grow at an average rate of around 11 per cent per year. This is what the Australian share market has achieved over the long term. (There are ways to earn even higher returns — which involve additional risks — and I will look at risk and return in chapter 4.)

In real life, the returns will vary from year to year. For example, my daughter was born in late 1994, and in the 15 years from the end of 1994 to the end of 2010 the returns from the broad Australian share market have averaged more than 10 per cent per year, and that is including the big loss of 40 per cent in 2008 in the global financial crisis. As this plan for our kids is going to span many decades, we can expect to have the odd bad year or so from time to time, but average returns of around 11 per cent are more than achievable by sticking to the plan. This is discussed further in chapters 4, 5 and 6.

There are many ways to get to the $1 million target more quickly or to reach a bigger target. But for now I'll just stick to the basic plan — starting with $1 in the account when the child is born. Starting with just $1, the basic plan involves making a contribution of $31 per month and increasing the monthly contribution by 3 per cent each year to stay ahead of inflation.

Table 1.1 shows what the investment fund should look like over time.

Table 1.1: a child's investment fund with $1 per day contributions

Age	Contributions per month	Total contributions	Likely value of fund
5	$36	$1 993	$2 500
10	$45	$4 479	$7 600
15	$55	$7 539	$17 000
20	$65	$11 199	$33 000
25	$79	$15 579	$61 000
30	$94	$20 859	$110 000
35	$111	$27 074	$193 000
40	$131	$34 454	$336 000
45	$155	$43 154	$577 000
50	$182	$53 390	$985 000

Table 1.1 assumes contributions starting at the rate of $31 per month (because it's much more practical than depositing $1 per day) and assumes investment returns that average around 11 per cent per year. The plan also requires the monthly contributions to be increased each year to stay ahead of inflation. In the basic plan above, the contributions increase by 3 per cent each year and all fractions are rounded up to the nearest dollar. So, in the second year, the contributions rise

from $31 per month to $36 per month. You can see that by the time the child is 20 years old the parents and child have put in $11 200, but it would have compounded and grown to around $33 000!

The numbers in table 1.1 are also based on achieving average returns of 11 per cent each year. In practice, returns will vary from year to year, so these results are only approximate likely outcomes. There will be years when the fund rockets ahead of the plan, but also other years when the balance goes backwards. We discuss variations in returns further in chapters 4, 5 and 6.

It's important to keep in mind, however, that $1 million in 50 years' time is not going to be worth the same as $1 million today, because inflation will have eaten away at its value. Assuming inflation keeps running at its present rate of around 2.5 per cent per year, $1 million received in 50 years' time will have lost around 70 per cent of its value, so it would be the same as receiving about $300 000 today. This means that if we stick to the $1 per day plan without increasing the contributions, we will end up with $1 million, but it will 'only' be worth around $300 000 in today's dollars. For most families this is still a tremendous present for their kids, and it is certainly much better than having no plan at all. The effects of inflation are covered in more detail in chapter 4.

If we want to aim for $1 million *after* the effects of inflation, we need to aim for a target of around $3.4 million over the 50 years, because that will be worth the same as $1 million today if inflation continues at 2.5 per cent per year. Fortunately, it is possible to reach this amount, and we can still do it by starting out very small:

→ If we start out with $100, start the contributions at $70 per month, or a little over $2 per day, and increase the contributions by 7 per cent each year (to stay well ahead of inflation), over 50 years the fund would reach around $2 to $3.8 million, or over $1 million in today's dollars after inflation.

→   Alternatively, if we start out with $1000 in the account, contribute $70 per month, and increase the contributions by only 6 per cent each year (to stay ahead of inflation), and find another $100 to contribute each year (for example, a Christmas gift from grandparents), over 50 years the fund would reach around $3 to $3.5 million.

So there are a number of ways of achieving great results, even if we only start out small. These tiny contributions in the early years can make a huge difference to the value of the fund over the years. The main thing is to start small and stick to the plan. This is much better than starting big and not sticking to it. Start with just $1 and get the plan underway. Once you and your kids start to see the fund growing, this will motivate you to contribute more whenever you can.

It also helps to start early, which is why it's best to start when the kids are born. Let's go back to the original $1 per day plan for the following examples. If you delay starting until the child is 10 years old, the fund would only be worth around $330000 when they turn 50. (See the figures for age 40 in table 1.1.) Think about that for a minute—by missing the first 10 years of contributions (which are around $4500), the fund value at age 50 is a whopping $650000 less!

If the child is already, say, 10 years old and you want to start the plan now, you can still get back on track—start with $7600 in the account and begin the $1 per day plan from there (see the 10-year fund total in table 1.1). That $7600 gets you back on track for the $1 million and makes up for the $650000 you would otherwise have been short. Pretty good use of $7600 if you ask me—turning it into an additional

$650 000! If you don't have the $7600 to kick the plan off, you could start from scratch but put in $100 per month and then continue the plan from there. Then you're back on track to reach $1 million when the child is 50.

This book will help you wade through the different types of accounts and products on the market to find simple, low-cost, low-maintenance, tax-effective investments that will get you to $1 million. There are no tricks, get-rich-quick schemes or trading systems. I explain how to invest in shares without using managed funds or stockbrokers, or having to pick individual shares, and how to invest in property without borrowing, using negative gearing or having to worry about tenants. I also cover taxes, including ways of minimising them and the taxes that apply to kids. You'll also find out that, in fact, our kids receive tax refunds in most years if they invest in the right types of assets and use some simple legal tax breaks.

1.2 The hard parts of the plan

There are three hard parts of the plan:

→   making the commitment to start it

→   sticking to it

→   learning (with our kids) how to invest the money well.

There are many people who will probably say that the plan will never work, mainly because they can't believe it's so simple. These are the same people who are probably mortgaged to the hilt, spend more than they earn, struggle from payday to payday and are always worrying about having enough money to get by. They may even find themselves saying something like, 'It's only $1 — it won't matter if I skip a few contributions.' But if you make the commitment to stick to the plan, it will work.

It does get easier after a while, once you see the money growing. I'll never forget trying to explain to my daughter (who was 10 at the time) how her mother and I had put less than $4000 into the fund since she was born but it had grown into over $10 000. 'But where did the other $6000 come from? It must be magic!' she kept saying. I told her that it was just compounding — leaving the money in there, never spending it and reinvesting all the earnings.

Just stick to this plan and watch it work — and keep control of it yourself. You and your kids will learn about a whole range of simple, low-fee, low-cost, tax-effective ways to invest your fund for great long-term growth.

1.3 The rules

There are some ground rules with the $1 per day plan.

1   Make regular contributions.

2   Invest the money in growth assets.

3   Reinvest all investment earnings in the fund.

4   Never spend it.

Rule 1—make regular contributions

It's not practical to actually deposit $1 into an account every single day. Regular contributions should be set up — for example, $31 per month or $14 per fortnight. I will go through a number of ways to make this happen like clockwork each month or fortnight in chapter 2. I have also mentioned that the fund will grow much more quickly if the regular contributions each year are increased to keep ahead of inflation, and if additional one-off contributions are made when possible.

Rule 2—invest the money in growth assets

A wide range of investments is available, and in Parts III and IV I'll discuss the types of investments that work best for the fund. Parents (and the kids when they start to take over the process) will need to spend about one hour per month learning about and managing the investments. It doesn't need to be exactly one hour each month. For example, in my family I find it easiest to spend a few hours each school holidays, rather than doing it during the term. It's also possible to spend less time than this — some low-maintenance methods are outlined in chapter 3. But the aim is not just to build wealth for our kids, the aim is also to teach them how to look after it and keep it growing. So the time we put in along the way will reap big rewards later on.

The funds are invested in growth assets — primarily shares — and also property. I will explain how to invest in shares without using managed funds, and without financial planners or stockbrokers, and without investing directly in shares. You can also invest in property without borrowing or using negative gearing, and without having to worry about tenants. There are a number of simple, low-cost, tax-effective, low-maintenance, 'set-and-forget' investments that small investors can use.

Rule 3—reinvest all investment earnings in the fund

All income generated by the fund stays in the fund — all interest, dividends, distributions, capital gains and other income that is received from the investments. That way, the fund earnings grow by generating earnings of their own. The only reason money will need to be taken out is to pay tax on the investments. Tax can be kept to a minimum — and this is covered later in this book.

Rule 4—never spend it

Never spend this money—it's for the long term. By adhering to this rule our kids get to learn the difference between:

→ *investing*—putting money away for the long term, never to be spent

→ *savings*—putting money away to buy things later

→ *spending money*—for day-to-day purchases.

The money in the investment fund is not for buying boats, cars or houses, paying off the mortgage or paying for a holiday. Never spend it. By following this plan our kids can learn all sorts of financial techniques to help them avoid personal debts and to pay off their own home mortgage quickly.

If we never spend the money, what is the point of having it?

This money is there to buy something far more important than cars, boats and holidays—financial freedom for our kids. The $1 million fund will generate investment income that can grow each year, and the fund can keep growing in value. Let's say your child turns 50 and their fund has around $1 million in it from the $1 per day plan. At this point, they have some real choices in life. They could choose to:

→ work part-time or stop working altogether, and they could start living off the investment income from their fund. Their investment fund of $1 million could generate around $50 000 income per year and should still grow in value at around 5 per cent or more per year so that the income also grows each year.

→ invest the fund in a different way that could generate around $80 000 income to live on and still grow in value at around 3 per cent each year.

→ keep working and reinvesting all fund earnings back into the fund. If they continued to invest in growth assets, this would keep the fund growing at an average rate of around 12 per cent each year. And if they continue to reinvest all earnings, the fund could grow to around $2 million by age 57 or close to $3 million by age 60. Therefore, if they avoid living off the fund earnings until they turn 57, the fund should have doubled in size, to $2 million, and they could then retire on an income of at least $100 000 per year.

If the child chooses any of these options, they wouldn't actually be spending the investments or selling the investment assets, they would be living off the investment fund's earnings. The investment assets remain intact and keep growing in value for as long as they want them to. This is what I mean when I say, 'Never spend it.'

Money buys choices. The simple little plan for $1 per day plus an hour per month will give our kids real choices later in life. The kids will be able to choose to work because they want to — not because they have to.

1.4 As the kids grow up

There are three stages in the $1 per day plan:

→ birth to age 10

→ age 11 to age 20

→ age 21 onwards.

Stage 1—birth to age 10

In the first 10 years, put away $1 per day into the kids' funds and spend about an hour per month learning and managing the fund. Each year we increase the contributions to stay ahead of inflation. We also try to put additional money into the account whenever possible — for example, from Christmas and birthday presents. The fund is in the parents' names, but we are simply holding it on the child's behalf. If the kids do chores around the house, we can pay them pocket money and also say that we are putting money away in their investment fund. At this stage, we are responsible for the fund — investing the money in simple, low-cost, growth assets and learning more about investments. Our 10-year-old son is now at the end of stage one. He is aware that some money is going into a fund for him because we mention it occasionally and also because he hears his older sister talking about it.

Stage 2—age 11 to age 20

By the age of 10 the kids should have started to appreciate money and what it does. They are probably ready to begin helping us by looking at different investments and checking statements and some of the paperwork. During this stage we can also start handing the responsibility for the fund over to them. They can begin making regular contributions and learning to put money from chores or gifts into the three categories mentioned earlier — investing (for the long term), savings (for major items to buy later) and spending (for day-to-day items). They should also start to take an interest in how the investments are going and begin coming up with some ideas of their own — and lots of questions. We continue to spend an hour per month together on the investment planning, monitoring and learning. Our 16-year-old daughter is currently in stage two.

Stage 3—age 20 onwards

By stage 3 the kids should be ready to take over complete responsibility of the fund. They have learned about investing, saving and spending, and they have a good understanding of the investment rules and principles of the fund. They will have been contributing regularly to the fund for several years now—out of pocket money, then part-time jobs, then their full-time jobs as they enter the workforce.

What about superannuation?

This plan does not take the place of superannuation. My kids will still be able to receive all the benefits of super later on. Indeed, super has its uses and should form a major part of their investments later on in life, but they shouldn't rely on super. Having super will not teach kids how to be financially smart. Many retirees today use their super payout at retirement to pay off their mortgage. In fact, this is one of the reasons for people taking on larger and larger mortgages when they are in their 40s and 50s—because they know they can pay part of it off with their super payout when they retire. However, once they have done this they have to rely on the government age pension for the rest of their lives, which could be another 30 or 40 years. That's not what super was intended for. The super system is teaching bad financial habits instead of good ones.

According to superannuation industry statistics, before compulsory super was introduced in 1992, 76 per cent of pension-age people were on the government pension. The compulsory super system was introduced in order to get this percentage down by helping more people save for their own retirement. But it has done the opposite—20 years after compulsory super was introduced the percentage of people on the government pension has increased to more than 80 per cent of pension-age people. A greater percentage of people now are relying on the age pension than ever before, so the super system is not doing its job. We are going to need to have a plan other than compulsory super to stay off the government pension.

Besides, under the current rules, our kids will need to wait until they are at least 60 years old before they can access their super. However, the $1 per day plan should enable them to retire or semi-retire much earlier if they want to. As well, the government is gradually increasing the age at which people can access their super. Who knows, in 40 or 50 years' time, the government might have shifted the age limit up to 65 or even 70.

1.5 Paying back our loan

As mentioned earlier, by sticking to the $1 per day contributions we are putting in about $7500 over the first 15 years. When the kids agree to take over the plan, they also agree to repay this loan when they turn, say, 40.

Going back to table 1.1 (on page 8), which is based on contributions remaining at $31 per month and assumes that investment returns average 11 per cent per year, the total fund balance when the child is 40 will be around $330 000. This money has come from two sources: contributions and reinvested income — $34 000 (in total contributions over the 40 years) + about $296 000 (reinvested earnings) = $330 000.

Only 5 per cent of the fund value is the money put in as contributions. The other 95 per cent has been generated through continually reinvesting the earnings back into the fund. If our loan of $7500 is repaid at this point, it would reduce the fund balance by $7500 — so the impact is less than 2 per cent of the fund balance, enabling the fund to continue on its path to $1 million.

The $7500 repaid in 40 years is not going to be worth the same as it is worth today, because inflation will have eaten away at its buying power. But this shouldn't be a concern because you will have learned to build the family budget around the $1 per day contributions. Think of that lost buying power of our $1 per day contributions as our 'gift' to the kids.

Why not make our contribution a gift instead of a loan?

There are several good reasons for making our contribution a loan instead of a gift:

→ It teaches the kids that there is no such thing as a free ride in life.

→ A loan sounds more commercial and more of a commitment if they actually have to pay it back.

→ It gives them an added incentive to continue with the plan and grow the fund, because they know they have to repay the $7500. The bigger they can grow the fund, the less of an impact repaying the loan will have on the fund.

When the loan is repaid, some of the things we could do with it include:

→ shouting ourselves (or the kids) a holiday or gift

→ leaving it in the kids' fund so it keeps growing

→ putting it towards the kids' mortgage, if they still have one

→ using it to start an investment fund for our grandkids

→ using it to help out other kids less fortunate than our own (and even get a tax deduction for it if we donate to a registered charity).

1.6 The kids won't learn this at school

Did you learn about investing and building wealth at school? I didn't either. I went to six primary schools and six high schools all over Australia (and a couple in the US) and I can't recall ever learning about investing and building wealth. My kids are going to two different schools in Sydney and they aren't learning about it there either. If you have kids at school already, are they learning about it? Probably not. Teachers are told to teach kids to study for exams, get the best marks they can, go to university if they get in, study the best course that their exam marks get them into, find a job for the next 30 or 40 years and hope that it's something they enjoy doing. The theory is, the better the exam marks, the better course you get into. And the more money you make, the happier you will be. Unfortunately, that's not how the real world works.

Working pays the bills but it doesn't build wealth. The jobs people have and how much they earn have very little to do with how wealthy they are. Neither does intelligence or a high IQ. Some of the wealthiest people in Australia were high school dropouts or barely finished high school. At the same time, our schools and universities are full of teachers, lecturers and professors with PhDs and super-high IQs — but teaching remains one of the lowest paid jobs in Australia. My plumber probably earns more than my kids' school principal or a university professor. But my plumber and the school principal or professor all have an equal chance of building real wealth for themselves and their kids.

Kids certainly don't learn about saving and investing from watching television either. They are bombarded with advertisements to get them to spend, spend, spend. It's up to us, the parents, to show them and teach them a different way.

1.7 What does 'wealth' mean?

When I say 'wealth', I'm talking about financial wealth. There are many other types of wealth that we wish for our kids — happiness, health, emotional and spiritual.

Happiness and satisfaction are not derived from a high income or a large amount of money. Unexpectedly receiving a large amount of money — for example, from a lottery win or inheritance — rarely ends with happiness all around. Indeed, too often it ends up in arguments, lawsuits and family break-ups.

Being wealthy has nothing to do with the amount of income we earn. In many cases, people who earn high incomes also have high expenses. They tend to live in expensive houses, drive expensive cars, go on expensive holidays, pay expensive school fees for their kids and have lots of expensive 'toys'. But how many of them actually have no mortgages, no car loans or leases, no boat loans, no personal loans and no credit card debt? How many of them paid cash for everything they own, including their house? Probably only a tiny percentage. In order to fund these expensive lifestyles, people on high incomes also tend to have big mortgages or second mortgages, big car loans, big boat loans, big personal loans and big credit card balances.

Are they wealthy? Probably not, because they couldn't survive for long if they lost their high-paying jobs. If the high income suddenly stopped, the banks, the credit card companies and all the other lenders would be on their back in a flash.

Are they happy? Not necessarily. They probably work too hard, and they may have to work long hours to pay for all those high living expenses and to make payments on all those loans. Because they work so hard, their health probably suffers and they probably don't eat enough good food or get enough exercise to take care of themselves for the long term.

Happiness most often comes from having control over our lives — being able to decide what we want to do, and when and how. With the $1 per day plan our kids can generate real wealth and at the same time develop the skills they need to manage money and make it work for them — so they will have more control over their lives. Being financially wealthy means having enough investments that generate investment income to pay for all our living expenses, so we can do what we really want to do with our lives. If you want to lie around a pool or on a big boat sipping martinis for the rest of your life, then being wealthy means having enough investments that allow you to do this. Or you may want to do something more meaningful with your life (after a couple of weeks sipping martinis on a big boat, of course!). You might decide that you want to leave your current lifestyle altogether and live in disadvantaged communities providing medical, educational or social assistance.

Or it may be something in-between these two extremes, perhaps taking up something you did many years ago, such as learning an instrument or writing, and maybe helping out in the local community or charities.

Or it could be a combination of all these things. That's the great benefit of financial wealth — it means we have control and can choose to spend our lives doing what's really important to us.

1.8 How much is 'wealthy'?

There are many 'how-much-is-enough' calculators available on websites and in books. They are generally based on our financial situation in retirement and assume that our living expenses once we finish work are going to be around 60 per cent to 70 per cent of our current living expenses. Don't make this assumption. There are also many books that recommend 'down-shifting' to a more self-sufficient lifestyle — for example, growing your own vegetables, making your own clothes and so on. But you may not want to do this. You may want to live in a way that is more expensive than the way you live now.

We're only on this planet once so we shouldn't spend our time doing something we don't absolutely love doing. Take some time to decide what's important to you and what you would really like to do with your life if you had the choice and the financial backing to do it. Then estimate how much that will cost — allowing for extras because everything always ends up costing more than you think! Include all the day-to-day expenses, such as food and clothing, as well as annual items, such as holidays, and other expenses you may only incur every few years, such as upgrading the car. For example, if you are planning to buy a $40 000 car every 10 years, you should include $4000 per year in the annual expense estimate. Better make it $5000 per year, to allow for inflation. Don't include any income you might generate in your ideal future life because you don't want to have to rely on it. This income is a bonus.

Once you have estimated your living expenses in your ideal future life, you can estimate how much investment capital is required to finance them. If your living expenses in your ideal future life are $50 000 per year, you will need investments of around 20 times that $50 000 — that is, $1 million. This $1 million in investment capital can do three things:

1   generate investment income of around 5 per cent ($50 000 per annum) after tax

2   leave your investment capital intact (so it lasts forever)

3   continue to grow in value — so your investment income can also grow each year — to counter the effects of inflation.

If you use a multiple of 20 times your annual expenses, you should never have to spend or eat into your investment assets. Remember, one of the rules in the $1 per day plan is that the investment fund is never cashed in or spent.

There are many 'retirement' tables and calculators that use other multiples such as 15 times or even as little as 10 times the annual living expenses. Most of these calculations want to know your current age because they assume that you will also be eating into your investment capital and running it down to zero by the time you're scheduled to die, according to the statistical life expectancy tables.

But you or your kids don't want to eat into the investment capital and run it down until you are scheduled to die! What if you live 10 years longer than the statistical tables say? What if you want to leave some money for the kids or grandkids after you've gone? What if you are going to need funds for major medical expenses? What if you want to lend or give some money to your kids to help them buy a house? What if you want to pay off their university debts for them? What if you want to buy a holiday home on the coast? What if you want to set up a charitable foundation?

We and our kids should plan to have enough investment capital to cover our living expenses out of investment income alone, and still have the investment capital remaining intact and growing for as long as we want it to. That's why a figure of at around 20 times your living expenses should be used as the minimum amount of capital needed.

In estimating how much you and your family have in investment capital, you need to add up all your investment assets and then deduct all your debts and liabilities. The following should be included as investment assets:

→ superannuation

→ shares

→ managed funds

→ investment properties (but be careful estimating values — if the properties include home units bought 'off the plan' in the last few years they may be worth a lot less than the purchase price)

→ savings and education bonds

→ vested shares or options in the company you work for that can be exercised now — and don't forget to deduct any tax payable

→ other investments.

The following items should not be included because they are not investments:

→ money saved to pay upcoming bills or expenses, or to pay for a holiday or a new television, and so on

→ your own business, if you work in it yourself. (In general, a business only has a value to someone else if you have managers running it for you)

→ your house — it's not an investment unless it's rented out

→ your holiday house — it's only an investment if it's rented out

→ cars, boats or household items — they are not investments, because they don't appreciate in value or generate income

→ tax liabilities.

Add all the investment assets up to find the total and then subtract all debts.

Debts may include:

→ mortgages and home loans

→ investment property loans

→ lines of credit

→ overdrafts

→ margin loans

→ credit cards

→ car or boat loans

→ personal loans

→ store discount cards

→ 'buy-now-pay-nothing-for-two-years' loans on household goods

→ money owed to friends and family

→ loans from business partners

→ any loans or debts you signed as 'guarantor'

→ any other loans or debts owed.

Total investment assets minus total debts equals your net investment assets. If you have enough net investment assets to cover 20 times all your expected living expenses in your ideal future life, you are financially wealthy.

Most Australian families have negative net investment assets using this test. It's a tough test because it doesn't count the family home as an investment asset (because it doesn't generate income), but it does include the home mortgage as a 'debt'. The test does this because, in order to be truly wealthy and spend your life doing what you really want to do, you don't want to have to sell your house and move into a much cheaper house in a cheaper part of the country.

If the family has negative net investment assets, there is no need to panic just yet. There is still time to do something about it. And the great news is that your kids have about 30 years more than you have to get their financial affairs in order.

The plan set out in this book will help you as parents give your kids a supreme gift — the knowledge, skills and money to be financially wealthy — so they can follow their dreams and do what they really want to do. But we need to start while they are still young, so the kids have time on their side.

Part II

GET
READY

Chapter 2

Finding $1 per day

2.1 Bringing up kids in Australia is expensive

It seems like every month or so there is a story on the television news, on current affairs shows or in the newspapers that adds up the total costs of bringing up kids in Australia. The total numbers look really scary. Depending on which study you read, the total cost per child adds up to anywhere between $300 000 and $750 000 from a child's birth to the time they leave university. The costs include food, clothing, school uniforms, books, holidays, toys, haircuts, medicines, a bigger house with more bedrooms, higher council rates, more water, gas and electricity, and so on. Despite all of these studies and news stories, people still have kids! The thought of changing nappies may scare some people off, but the cost of around $500 000 doesn't seem to!

The size of families has been reducing over the last 100 years. Growing up in the 1930s and 1940s, my father was one of 10 kids in his family. Growing up in the 1960s and 1970s I was one of four kids in my family. Now, in the 1990s and 2000s, my wife and I have only two kids. So with fewer kids per family these days, there should be more to share around.

Also, in previous generations people had kids much earlier in their adult lives. A hundred years ago people started having kids at around 16 to 20 years of age. Fifty years ago it was around 22 to 25 years of age. Today, many people have kids when they are in their 30s or 40s — after both parents have established careers and have been working for many years. Therefore, the parents of today should have accumulated many more financial resources to fund the expenses of having children.

In previous generations, most families had only one 'bread-winner'. Today, after the kids start school, around 75 per cent to 80 per cent of mothers go back into the workforce. For families where either one or neither parent works, there are numerous government benefits available — none of which were around 100 years ago.

Despite all this, bringing up kids in Australia is expensive, and many families today struggle from payday to payday to make ends meet. This chapter explores some of the ways to find that $1 per day.

2.2 Government assistance

There are a number of government schemes that provide financial assistance to families including:

→ baby bonus payments

→ family tax benefits

→ child care benefits

→ child care rebates

→ parenting payments

→ carer payments and carer allowances

→ dependent rebates and offsets

→ large family supplement and multiple birth allowances

→ rent assistance

→ medical expenses tax offset.

The names and details are constantly changing, so check these websites:

→ Family Assistance Office: <www.familyassist.gov.au>

→ Centrelink: <www.centrelink.gov.au>

→ Australian Tax Office: <www.ato.gov.au>.

2.3 Lost superannuation and unclaimed money

Since 1992 it has been compulsory for employers to pay superannuation for all workers aged between 18 and 70 who earn more than a minimum amount per month. Even before it became compulsory, many employers were doing it voluntarily, especially large companies and government departments.

The problem is that many employees change jobs and lose track of their super funds over the years, because each employer will put money into a different super fund. It is not uncommon for people to have half-a-dozen super accounts from previous jobs. When I wrote the first edition of this book in 2006 there was $8 billion in lost super accounts, but by 2010 the total had grown to $13 billion. That's an average of $1000 per adult in Australia.

Several years ago I saw an article in a newspaper about lost super and decided to give it a try. I filled in a few forms (for myself and my wife) and sent them away. A couple of months later the service I used wrote back and said that they had found $658 in lost super for my wife, so we put it into our super fund.

It is estimated that around one-third to half of all working Australians have money sitting in these lost super accounts, of which there are 5.4 million. If your family has two working parents, the chances are that one or both of you will have a lost super account somewhere. It's well worth making the effort to track it down. There are several services that can help you do this, including:

→ Australian Taxation Office Lost Members Register — visit <www.australia.gov.au/service/superseekers-lost-superannuation.search>.

→ Find My Super — visit <www.findmysuper.com.au>.

When you find this money, you can't take it in cash. It's superannuation, so it has to go into your main super fund until you retire. But it's still worth tracking down.

Aside from lost super, there are several other places that lost or unclaimed money can be found. Unlike super, when you track down any other unclaimed money you can usually take it in cash, or put it into the kids' funds. Try these sources:

→ Australian Securities and Investments Commission (AISC) — visit ASIC's 'Fido' service at <www.fido.gov.au>.

→ You can also track down lost or unclaimed money held by the governments of the states where you've lived. The departments in each state have different titles, but try a web search using the terms 'state revenue office', 'state treasury', 'public trustee' and 'finance department' together with the name of the state.

2.4 Other ways to find $1 per day

Here are some simple strategies that can help you to save money — and even to find money you probably didn't realise you had!

→ *Choose generic brands.* When you do the supermarket shopping, consider buying generic brands instead of the more expensive brand names. It's worth remembering that both are often produced by the same manufacturer.

→ *Bypass the bottled water.* It will probably come as a shock to you when I tell you that bottled water is more expensive per litre than the oil that fuels your car! If you buy it (and soft drinks) regularly, you will be amazed at how much you can save by drinking tap water instead or investing in a water filter.

→ *Cut back on smoking.* If you're a smoker, another way to find $1 per day is by spending less on cigarettes. I'm not suggesting that smokers need to stop altogether and put the whole amount saved into their child's investment account — but $1 per day's worth is just a couple of cigarettes! (If you did decide to give up smoking, the savings — quite apart from the health benefits — would be astronomical.)

→ *Put your non-smoker's bonus to work.* Non-smokers generally pay several hundred dollars per year less for life insurance than smokers. If this applies to you and your partner, one option is to spend part of this saving on yourselves and to put part of it straight into your child's investment account.

→ *Don't gamble it all away.* Australians are among the biggest gamblers in the world. The Australian Productivity Commission reported in 2010 that Australians lose more than $19 billion on all forms of gambling per year. That's more than 3 per cent of all household spending, and it averages an incredible $1500 per adult per year. We spend a lot more than this amount; this is just the net *losses* on gambling. I'm not saying that everyone should stop all forms of gambling. But we should decide which things we are doing for a bit of fun and social interaction, and which things are just a waste of money — money that could help secure our kids' future.

→ *Stockpile loose change.* It's surprising how loose change mounts up, and it can make a very useful contribution to the $1 per day fund. Here are some of the places we regularly find loose change at our house: in pockets, under lounge suite cushions, under car seats, and in bags and suitcases that have been stored away. If you get the kids involved, you'll probably be surprised at how much they come up with. Our kids know that our wallets and purses are out of bounds, of course, but everything else they find — plus the loose change I'm in the habit of depositing on a table near the front door at the end of each day — is 'fair game' as long as it goes into their investment account.

2.5 Parents' commitment for the first 10 to 15 years

Until the kids are around 10 years old, the parents are responsible for all aspects of the $1 per day plan. When they reach this age the kids can start to make contributions of their own (from chores or pocket money) and also start to get involved by helping to manage and invest the money, but the parents can continue with the regular contributions. From around age 15 the kids can probably commit to taking over the $1 per day contributions. At this age most kids will start to get part-time work outside the home and will have learned to put the first few dollars out of every pay packet into the investment fund. If the kids are not working while they are in school, the parents simply continue to make the $1 contributions until they do begin to earn money.

If parents contribute to the $1 per day plan for the first 15 years by starting out with $31 per month, then increasing by 3 per cent each year for inflation, the contributions add up to a total of around $7500. I don't think about the $1 per day commitment as a $7500 lump sum that my wife and I had to find over 15 years. I prefer to think of it as $1 per day. Don't let the total put you off just because it sounds like a lot of money. All you have to think about is that $1 you're going to find today. And remember that the $1 per day per child over the first 15 years is a loan, and is expected to be repaid when the child reaches a particular age.

2.6 Salary deductions and direct debits

Finding $1 per day in loose change is useful, but it clearly has limits. In the meantime, parents need a simple way of putting away the $1 per day from the child's birth, without having to think about it.

The most effective way is to set up regular direct debits. If you are paid by direct credit to a bank account, the best way is to ask your employer to pay part of your monthly or fortnightly pay directly into the kids' accounts and the rest into the parents' bank account. Most employers with automated payrolls, such as medium and large businesses, and most government departments, can do this. If the employer is unable or unwilling to do this — for example, if it is a small business, or if the parents themselves operate a small business — the next best way is to set up a regular direct debit from the parents' main bank account into the kids' accounts. It's simple to do this, and your bank will tell you how.

I recommend making the monthly contribution $31 rather than $30, or the fortnightly contribution $16 instead of $14, as these unusual amounts stand out on a statement, and they are also a 'painless' way of getting ahead of the $1 per day target.

The beauty of a direct salary deduction or direct debit from the bank account straight into the kids' account is that we never even know it's gone. We don't get our hands on it so we don't get the chance to spend it. If it automatically goes into the kids' accounts, it's amazing how people simply adjust their spending habits without even thinking about it.

Increasing the contributions each year

Each year we should try to increase the contributions to the kids' accounts to keep ahead of inflation. If we were to increase them by 5 per cent each year, in the first year we would contribute $1 per day or $31 per month, and the following year we would increase it to $1.05 per day or $32.50 per month (or round it up to $33). The year after that we would increase it to $1.10 per day or $34 per month and so on. In this way our kids can end up with much more than $1 million in the fund in 50 years, but it will be worth $1 million in today's dollars. I covered a number of different ways of doing this in chapter 1, and inflation is covered in greater detail in chapter 4.

2.7 Budgets

If you are having trouble finding that $1 per day, you may need to try doing a budget. Everybody hates budgets but they are a great way to track down where all the money goes. There are several good budgeting tools available on the web and in your local library (including my other books!).

However, because we are just talking about a tiny $1 per day, you will probably find that if you just set up an automatic salary deduction or direct credit into your child's account for $31 per month, you won't even notice any change in your day-to-day living expenses.

2.8 Grandparents—do it for your grandkids

The $1 per day plan is also a great way for grandparents to get involved in their grandkids' futures. There are a number of ways they can do this. For example, they might decide to be the ones to put in the $1 per day for the first 10 to 15 years, which the kids will eventually pay back. Many would then enjoy spending time with the grandkids working on the investment plan, whether in person or by email. Or they might be happy to contribute, say, $1000 as a lump sum to start the fund off, and the parents then contribute the $1 per day. Or they can make a contribution by giving a gift of money a couple of times a year, such as at birthdays and Christmas — or perhaps even setting up a regular payment via salary deduction or direct debit.

2.9 Time to set goals

I'm a great believer in 'everything in moderation'. You don't have to completely change your lives to get this plan underway for the kids. I'm not talking about 'downshifting' to the country, growing your own vegetables, home-schooling the kids and making your own clothes. This is too radical and doesn't suit many families — mine in particular! All I'm talking about is looking at some of the little things you spend money on and making a few adjustments so you can free up $1 per day for your child's future.

Close your eyes, take a deep breath and say to yourself, 'My child's financial future deserves $1 per day. We are going to start the plan today and we are going to do whatever it takes to make it happen.' If you make this commitment to yourself, you'll find that you will make it happen. Set up the salary deduction or direct debit from your bank account. Don't get carried away with a $5 per day plan or a $10 per day plan to get to the $1 million in a much shorter time. Just make it $1 per day initially. If you take this first step, you will find yourself adjusting pretty quickly — looking for cheaper alternatives and cutting down on low-priority luxuries when you need to.

This book does not list hundreds of different ways to save money — you will find the ways that are relevant to your family's situation. Every time you receive the statements regarding the kids' investment accounts, it will inspire you to stick to the plan and find ways to contribute even more to the fund.

With this plan, you can give your kids $1 million and also give them the knowledge and skills to be able to manage money and make it grow — but it won't happen by accident. You will need a plan and you need to stick to it. While the kids are very young you are in charge of starting the plan and getting it underway, and you will need to set goals to keep the plan on track.

Long-term goals set the 'big picture'. They remind us of what we're aiming for in the future and why it's going to be worth the effort. Medium-term goals are good checkpoints along the way to make sure we're on the right track. Short-term goals help us keep focused on what we have to do right now to keep the plan working. Goals are always more effective if we actually write them down and sign them; an example is shown below.

Long-term goal

Target date: June 2060 (e.g. child's 50th birthday)

I/We _____ and _____

(parents' full names) agree to give _____

_____ (kids' names)

$1 million each by investing $1 per day and one hour per month of my/our time, so they can be financially independent and have real choices later in life.

Medium-term goals

Target date: 31 December 2011 (e.g. one year from today)

Reach a balance of $500 in the fund(s) (from contributions plus interest). Make the fund's first investment using cash in the cash account.

Short-term goals

Target date: 1 January 2011 (e.g. 30 days from today)

➢ Open a cash account for each child.

➢ Set up salary deductions or direct debits into the cash accounts.

➢ Open an online broker account for each child.

➢ Set aside one hour next week to learn more.

The $1 per day plan does work. But to achieve the goal you need to start the plan and stick to it. If you are serious about starting this plan for your kids, try this first test — put your hand into your pocket or handbag right now and find $1. This will be your first dollar toward the $1 million target. If you couldn't find $1, only $5 or $10, this is even better. But it only takes $1 to start. If you did find that first dollar, you have what it takes to do all the other steps in the plan. Keep this first dollar and put it somewhere where you will see it every day. Use it as a reminder to stick to the goals you have written down. You may want to frame this first dollar to show the kids how it all started.

Part III

GET
SET

Chapter 3

Getting started

If you've made it this far into the book, you've made the commitment to put aside $1 per day for each child in your family. Congratulations! Perhaps you've also decided to kick the fund off with an initial contribution, such as a gift of $100 or so from a grandparent or perhaps part of a tax refund. The more there is at the start, the bigger and faster the investment will grow. You've also made the decision to set up a salary deduction or direct debit from your bank account. In part III I will go through the features required to get the investment plan started and I introduce the next two building blocks.

Figure 3.1: basic building blocks

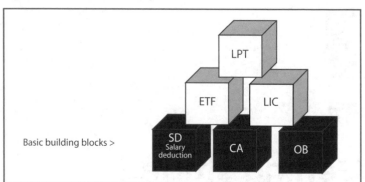

3.1 What about paying off our debts first?

Before opening cash or online broker accounts for the kids, the first thing to think about is the family's financial situation overall. There is a very sound theory that says that, before we start to invest any spare cash, we should pay off any debts that are not tax-deductible. Such debts include loans taken out to fund purchases that don't earn income — like the home mortgage, car loans, boat loans, personal loans and money owed on credit cards. The interest on these loans is not tax-deductible, whereas the interest on loans taken out to purchase income-producing investments such as property or shares generally is tax-deductible. These two types of debt are sometimes called 'bad debt' and 'good debt' respectively.

We should generally pay off the non–tax-deductible (bad) debt with the highest interest rate first if we have any spare cash. Once these debts are paid off, the debts with lower interest rates, such as personal and car loans, should be paid off. The home mortgage should be paid off last. Only then should we start investing any spare cash. That said, we need to weigh this up against the aim of starting a very small investment program for our children, knowing that the sooner we start the sooner it will grow to $1 million. After all, $1 per day won't break the bank — nor is it enough to fix the family's problems if debt is a serious issue. In this case I refer you to my book *101 Ways to Get Out of Debt*.

3.2 In whose name should accounts be opened?

When setting up the salary deduction or direct debit from your bank account, the first thing you will be asked for by the payroll department or bank is the details of where the money is to be paid — that is, the name of the account, the bank or financial institution, and the account number.

One decision to make at the outset is whose name to put the accounts and investments in — the name of the parent or parents or the child's name? Generally, you should try to put the investment in the name of the person in the lowest tax bracket. That way, less of the investment income and gains are paid in tax and more of it can be reinvested.

Later in this chapter I outline the special rules that apply to tax on kids and their investment income. But first, there are a couple of practical issues to consider. Most banks and financial institutions don't allow children below a certain age to open and operate accounts on their own.

Different banks have different age cut-offs. You could put the accounts in the name of the parent or parents, and simply tell yourselves that this money is really for the child. However, if it's in the parents' names, it may get confusing when there are different accounts for each child. Also, parents may be tempted to use the money in 'emergencies'. If the kids' names appear on the accounts, it is much more likely that the parents will think twice before spending it.

Having the kids' names on the accounts is also very motivating — for them and for us as parents. The kids will get a buzz out of getting paperwork in the mail and seeing their investment grow, and this will spur them on to invest more money and make it grow faster. They will take more of an interest in it, and help check the statements and choose investments.

Another outcome of putting the investments in the kids' names is that if we get into trouble with creditors, the kids' funds are out of reach. The funds in the accounts belong to the kids, not the parents. This way the kids' future financial wellbeing is not jeopardised by any credit or other legal problems the parents may have.

The most common way for accounts to be held for children is to put them in the name of the parent or parents 'in trust for' each child so that the child's and parents' names appear on the account. This way everyone can see that it is the child's account, so there is no confusion.

There are a few ways the accounts can be put in the name of the parent(s) in trust for the child. If the parents' names are John Stephen Smith and Mary Jane Smith, and the child's name is Junior Monty Smith, the account could be named:

→ John Stephen Smith In Trust For Junior Monty Smith

→ Mary Jane Smith In Trust For Junior Monty Smith

→ John Stephen Smith and Mary Jane Smith In Trust For Junior Monty Smith.

Financial institutions will allow most accounts to be opened in parents' names 'in trust for' a child's name. These include banks, building societies, cash trusts, managed funds, stock-broker accounts, shares and so on. Application forms for opening accounts will generally include specific instructions for opening accounts 'in trust for' someone else. In fact, most of the wealth in Australia is held in accounts that are owned by trustees 'in trust' for beneficiaries (including all super-annuation funds and managed funds), so all types of financial institutions deal with accounts held in trust every day.

If the bank has a rule preventing trust names in the account, the account can be named in the following ways:

→   John Stephen Smith <Junior Monty Smith A/c>

→   Mary Jane Smith <Junior Monty Smith A/c>

→   John Stephen Smith and Mary Jane Smith
      <Junior Monty Smith A/c>.

Once the account name has been decided, stick to that exact name for all other accounts and all other documents relating to that child.

3.3 One parent or both parents?

One advantage of having both parents' names on the account (in trust for the child) is that either parent can operate the account — but make sure that the application form specifies 'either to sign' the account.

On the other hand, having both parents' names on the account means that they both need to sign documents from time to time. Even if 'either to sign' is specified on the application form, there are times when both parents will be asked to sign. For example, when setting up direct credit authorities with employers and share registries it is often a requirement that both parents sign the account, even though the bank has been told that either parent can operate the account.

Another advantage of having both parents' names on the account and both parents needing to sign for transactions is that it is a safeguard against one parent being tempted to withdraw from the account for emergencies or unnecessary luxuries.

Also keep in mind that financial institutions get very picky about changing names on accounts after they have been opened. It often takes a long time (and lots of paperwork) to get all the names on all the accounts to match up exactly (spelling, capitals, initials, spaces between letters). By having the parents' name on the account, the child cannot close it or withdraw money by himself or herself. You may trust them not to do something as silly as that, but you'd be surprised what kids get up to when they get together with their friends. Kids will sometimes tell their friends their PIN or passwords just to prove that they know them.

3.4 Trustee and beneficiary

When one person (in this case a parent) holds an asset (like a bank account, shares or another investment) 'in trust for' someone else (the child), that person is known as the 'trustee' and the child is the 'beneficiary' of that asset.

The trustee is the legal holder of the asset and operates the account. In this case, the parent is the legal owner, but acts as the trustee. Any benefits that arise from the investment — such as income, interest, dividends and so on — are held for the beneficiary. The trustee cannot spend the money — it doesn't belong to them, it must be held for the benefit of the child. So, for example, any income from investments held in trust for the child is not counted as income of the parent, it is counted as belonging to the child. Likewise, when investments are sold, the money received from the sale does not belong to the parent, it belongs to the child and must stay in the child's fund.

The beneficiary is the person who receives the benefit of any investments held in trust for them. Even though it is the parent as trustee who buys the investments and signs the paperwork, the child receives the income and other benefits from the investment. There is no special 'trust deed' that needs to be signed in order to set up this trustee–beneficiary relationship. Opening an account in the name of a parent or parents 'in trust for' a child establishes the trustee relationship.

If you did want to set up a formal trust deed, this could be done by a lawyer. There are a number of situations you might want to cover in the trust deed; for example:

→   at what age the child is to receive the money (for example, some parents specify that the child must graduate from university or join the family business in order to receive the money)

→   what happens in the event of divorce or separation of the parents

→   what happens to the money in the event of the death of the child

→   what happens if the child runs off and marries someone the parents don't approve of.

In the case of our kids, my wife and I have kept the trusts as simple as possible, with no trust deeds. In our view, the money is not ours to give them if they behave and do the 'right thing'. It is their life and their money. Our role as parents is to give them the knowledge and skills to learn to make their own decisions. And the child makes most of the contributions to the fund, because after the age of 10 or so they start to put their own money in.

3.5 Tax on kids

When we open accounts and investments in trust for a child, the money and any income from it are the child's income, not ours, so it's important to know a bit about how kids are taxed. This section is not intended to provide comprehensive tax advice; it merely outlines some of the current rules. Check with your accountant or tax agent, if you have one, because tax laws and tax rates are always changing and each family may have particular circumstances that affect how the tax laws apply to them. The ATO website <www.ato.gov.au> contains current tax rates and the current rules relating to taxes on kids.

Children are taxed in various ways in Australia, depending on the type of income they have.

Gifts

Gifts made to children are generally not classed as 'income', so they are usually not taxed. When Grandma gives Junior $50 at Christmas, this is not classed as income, so Junior does not have to declare it as income and pay tax on it. When you set up the salary deduction or direct debit to transfer money directly into Junior's account, that is a loan and Junior doesn't pay income tax on it. If you decided to make your contributions a gift instead of a loan, that gift is not taxable either. Pocket money paid to children is generally tax-free also.

Hobby income

If Junior collects cricket cards or Barbie dolls and sells some to make a bit of extra money, this is usually called hobby income, so Junior is not taxed on any income he or she makes. Similarly, if Junior fixes bikes or skateboards for other kids every now and then, any cash he or she receives from this type of occasional activity would also usually be called hobby income and not be taxed. Likewise, if the kids set up a lemonade stand every now and then to make some extra cash, this will probably also be classed as a hobby, not a business or a regular job.

Earned income

If, on the other hand, Junior gets a regular job at the local hamburger joint for a few hours per week, or gets a regular job mowing lawns for neighbours, this is classified as 'earned income' and he or she will be taxed in the same way as you and I pay tax on income from working. The rules are vague, however, and it depends on the circumstances of each case. Take the case of lawnmowing — if Junior only did it once in a while for a couple of neighbours, this would probably be classed as hobby income and not taxed. But if he or she went about it in a businesslike manner, such as advertising in the local paper, buying fuel regularly, paying a couple of friends to help out and keeping records of jobs done, the tax office would probably start to say that the net income should be taxable, because Junior is really running a 'business'. There is a tax-free threshold (which, at the time of writing, is $6000 per annum) and also a 'low income tax offset' (a tax offset of $1500 for incomes up to $30000 at the time of writing), so kids may be able to earn up to $16000 in 'earned income' from regular jobs or real businesses before they start to pay income tax on it.

Investment income

Investment income is where it gets tricky. Any income received by children from investments — interest, dividends, rental income, or capital gains on the sale of shares or other assets — will be taxed at penalty rates of tax, meaning at a higher rate than adults. At the time of writing, the tax rules for children's investment income are as follows:

→ The first $416 in investment income is tax-free.

→ Investment income between $416 and $1307 (at the time of writing) is taxed at 66 per cent.

→ If investment income is over $1307, it is all taxed at the top marginal rate for adults, which is 45 per cent.

This all sounds nasty, but it is not as bad as it seems:

→ Our kids will be investing in Australian shares that pay 'franked' dividends and in property, which pays partly 'tax-deferred' distributions (these are discussed further in chapters 5 and 6), so the kids get tax credits for much of the income tax payable.

→ There is a 'low-income offset' that is available to all Australians earning low incomes and our kids can take advantage of this. At the time of writing, if their income is below $30 000, they will get a credit of up to $1500 on any tax payable.

→ Most of the investments will be in growth investments, so they will not generate much income each year. Investors don't get taxed when an investment grows in value each year, only when it generates income. (Capital growth and income are explored in greater detail in chapter 4.)

→ They will sell investment assets very rarely, so they won't be generating taxable capital gains very often.

→ If and when the kids do sell investments, they can take advantage of capital gains tax discounts. Only half the net gain is counted as taxable income if the asset has been owned for more than 12 months. This means that the tax rate on these capital gains is half the taxpayer's normal tax rate.

→ Low-income earners (which is mainly children and retirees) also avoid paying the Medicare levy of 1.5 per cent of taxable income, even though they are among the biggest users of doctors, medicines and other health services.

What does it all mean for our kids? The effects of these rules are:

→ For around the first 10 years of the $1 per day plan (or until the fund reaches around $8000), the kids should get tax refunds from the tax office each year.

→ For the next 20 years of the plan (or until the fund reaches around $100 000), they should generally not pay tax on investment earnings from the fund.

This seems too good to be true, but here's how it works: if the investments are mainly in Australian shares or Australian share funds (which they will be under our plan), the kids will receive tax refunds for franking credits each year from the tax office until the income starts to rise above $416 each year, which will usually not be until the fund starts to reach around $8000 or $9000. This would happen around year 10 with the $1 per day plan. In these first 10 years, then, the kids don't need to lodge tax returns until their investment income gets to be above $416, but they are allowed to apply for refunds of the franking credits on their dividends from shares.

From around years 10 to 20 on the $1 per day plan the investment income starts to reach more than $416 each year, so they will need to lodge tax returns. However, the kids can then use the 'low-income offset', which means that they pay no tax until their investment income reaches $3333 each year.

This will not occur until the investment fund reaches around $65 000, or around year 27 with the $1 per day plan.

Let's take a look at an example. Say you've been putting in the $1 per day since your child was born and 10 years later the fund is worth $8000. This money is invested in the following types of assets:

Australian shares $7000

Cash account   + $1000

Total fund $8000

The Australian shares are paying, say, 4 per cent 'fully franked' dividends per year and the cash account is paying 5 per cent interest per year. For that particular year the income would look like this:

Dividend income   = $7000 × 4%   = $280

plus franking credits   = $280 ÷ 70 × 30 = $120
(this will appear on the statement)

plus interest on cash   = $1000 × 5%   = $50

Total taxable income   = $450

The total taxable income is $34 above the $416 tax threshold, so the child pays the penalty 66 per cent tax on $34. The penalty tax = 66 per cent × $34 = $22. But they also get a credit for the $120 worth of 'franking credits' (because the companies the child invested in have already paid income tax on the company profits). But because of the low income tax offset, they would receive a tax refund of the full $120 in franking credits for that year.

By the way, this tax refund from the shares worth $7000 is equivalent to getting an additional return of 1.7 per cent after tax ($120 ÷ $7000) — on top of whatever return they are already getting from the investment. This means that, if the pre-tax return from the shares is, say, 11 per cent for the year before tax, the after-tax return would be 12.7 per cent for that year. Put that refund back into the fund each year and the fund will compound even faster!

So you need to get the kids a tax file number as soon as you can in order to receive the tax refund cheques and reinvest them in the fund.

Tax rules are constantly changing, so find out the latest details from the ATO website <www.ato.gov.au> or ask your tax agent or accountant.

3.6 Tax file numbers for the kids

Most kids don't have a tax file number (TFN) because their earned income is below the $6000 tax-free threshold and their investment income is below $416. But in our case the kids will be aiming to receive franking credits from the tax office each year, so it's necessary to apply for a TFN for each child.

Lodging tax returns

As I've mentioned, because of the low income tax offset the kids generally don't need to lodge tax returns until their income, 'investment income' (from interest and/or dividends) gets above $3333 each year. This means that, in the early years, they won't have to lodge a tax return. They will, however, want to get those franking credits. This can be done by lodging form NAT4098-6, which is called an Application for Refund of Franking Credits for Individuals and can be downloaded from the ATO website. Each child will need their own TFN to be able to lodge this form each year.

When to get a tax file number

The TFN should be obtained for each child before they are due to lodge their first tax return or apply for their first refund of franking credits. It's a good idea to do this straight after the kids' cash accounts are opened. Tax returns and applications for refund of franking credits can be lodged from the end of each financial year (June) until around March or April the following year (if a tax agent is used). In our case we want to get the tax refund as soon as possible (so they can reinvest it quickly), so the form for the kids should be lodged in July or August.

The TFN application form can be downloaded from the ATO website. The ATO will need to see the child's birth certificate and a copy of the bank account in their name. Attach these to the TFN application form, follow the other instructions on the form and send them in to the ATO.

Once the kids have their own TFNs, their tax returns or refund forms can be lodged after the end of each year to get their tax refunds if they have invested in shares that paid franked dividends. Keep all the dividend statements, because they will be needed when completing the tax refund form at the end of the year. Or give them to your tax agent or accountant at the end of the year. Don't forget that the cost of lodging tax returns is deductible, which will reduce their tax even further, or give them a bigger refund.

In reality, while the child's investments total less than around $500, they will not be receiving dividend income in the very early years if starting out with just $1. So it's not strictly necessary to get the TFN until it's time to lodge the tax return or refund form. But it's always better to get the TFN paperwork out of the way while you're setting up the other building blocks of the plan, and once it is done it's out of the way forever.

3.7 Cash account and online broker account

There are three basic building blocks in the $1 per day plan. For each child the following should be set up:

→ a cash account

→ a salary deduction (or direct debit) to transfer money into the cash account regularly

→ an online broker account that will be used to buy and sell investments.

Figure 3.2: basic building blocks

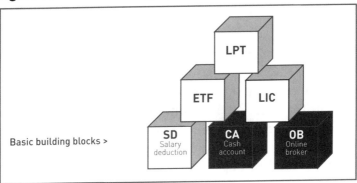

Each child should have their own online broker account, their own cash account linked to the broker account and their own salary deduction from your payroll or your main family bank account that puts money regularly into the cash account.

How it works

The online broker account, cash account and salary deduction go hand in hand. The salary deduction from your payroll or your main family bank account puts your regular contributions into the kids' cash account automatically each month. The cash account is linked to the online broker account so that when you buy shares using the online broker account, the money to buy the shares comes automatically out of the cash account. You can buy listed investments such as shares using your online broker account once the cash balance has grown to $500.

For example, let's say you want to use $1000 to buy shares or units in XYZ. You log on to the broker account and buy 1000 shares or units at, say, $1 each (a step-by-step guide for buying shares is provided in chapter 5). The brokerage on that 'buy' transaction would be about $20, depending on the broker's fee structure, so the total cost for that investment is $1020. The broker account will automatically take the $1020 cash from the linked cash account three business days later and use it to buy the shares or units in XYZ.

At the end of the month, the cash account statement will show that the balance has been reduced by $1020 and the broker account will show the investment in XYZ. It's as simple as that. You don't need to write cheques, fill in application forms or make phone calls. Once the cash account, broker account and salary deduction are set up and linked, you are ready to start the $1 per day plan.

Almost all online broker accounts come with their own in-house cash account automatically linked — this is the simplest approach. It would be ideal to get a good broker account and a good cash account at the same financial institution, and this is a good place to start. What we want is a good, low-cost broker account that comes automatically linked to its own internal cash account that pays high interest, has no minimum balance and no fees. Unfortunately, there are not many cash account and broker account combinations that offer the best of both worlds. There is generally a compromise in either the cash account or the broker account in these in-house broker/cash combinations, so it is generally possible to mix and match an online broker account from one institution with a cash account from another.

What to look for in an online broker account

The online broker account will be used to make it easy and inexpensive to buy investments, including share and property investments. It costs nothing to open an online broker account.

Don't worry — you won't be buying shares in individual companies for many years (perhaps never, if you would prefer not to). I'm not going to get you to start yelling, 'Buy BHP!' just yet. For the first few years a good online broker account is needed to buy many other types of investments for the kids' funds.

Most of the major online stockbroker services offer plenty of features for long-term investors like us. Many services also have lots of fancy extras that are purely for short-term traders, but we don't need those. The tests to find a suitable online broker account that work for the $1 per day plan are:

→   Low brokerage rates. The major online brokers charge between $20 and $30 per trade for small transactions (those less than around $10 000 per parcel, bought or sold). In the early years, however, you will be buying (and very rarely selling) parcels of around $500 to $1000.

→   No fees. Several of the brokers offer two or three different levels of service. For those people who want more features (mainly designed for short-term traders) there is usually a monthly or annual fee. All we need are the basic services with no regular fees (apart from the brokerage fee per trade).

→ Basic information for transactions. We need information such as the current price (some services only offer delayed prices with the basic service), market depth, order status, online contract notes and charting. These will be covered further in chapter 5.

→ Research database. Most online brokers have access to a great deal of information about listed companies, including balance-sheet data from the previous 10 years, profit and loss statements, dividend histories, announcements and so on. This will become vital later on if and when you start to buy direct shares — that is, shares in individual companies.

→ CHESS sponsorship. Many years ago shareholders used to receive a share certificate when they bought shares. Now we just receive a Clearing House Electronic Subregister System (CHESS) holding statement saying that we own shares in the company. There will be a CHESS application form as part of the paperwork to open the broker account.

→ Phone trades. All the online broker services have call centres and staff who can answer questions. Most of them allow buy and sell orders to be placed over the phone. However, the brokerage for phone orders is higher than for internet orders — about $60 per order. New investors may prefer to place their first orders over the phone because a staff member will be able to help out. But most people find very quickly that using the internet is much more convenient — we can see other buyers and sellers in the market, the order being processed and executed, and a contract note is sent virtually instantly.

Non-essential features that you may be interested in, but don't necessarily need are:

→ Access to international stock exchanges. Many online brokers offer direct access to major overseas markets such as New York, Tokyo and London. We are unlikely to need this for the kids' investment fund for many years, perhaps never.

→ Exchange-traded options. This feature is not necessary for the kids' investments.

→ Margin lending. This feature is not needed as the kids don't need to borrow money.

→ CFDs (Contracts for Difference). These are speculative bets that are not suitable for long-term investors. Be careful because CFD providers offer the lowest brokerage rates on share trading in order to lure people into the CFD trading trap. Most CFD providers offer brokerage on share trades of less than $20 per trade to lure you in. Don't take the bait.

Online broker services are offered by four different types of institutions in Australia:

1 All of the big banks in Australia (and a couple of the smaller ones) have online broker services. These are generally designed for individual investors like us.

2 Full-service stockbrokers (such as JB Were and Bell Potter) and most investment banks (such as Macquarie and the foreign investment banks) are generally set up for servicing institutional trading (big managed funds and superannuation funds), but also service high-net-worth private clients, and some also offer low-cost online broker services (but these are much more expensive for our plans).

3 Small independent online brokers (such as Morrison Securities)

4   CFD providers (such as CMC, IG, First Prudential, GFT). These are set up primarily to sell CFDs (contracts for difference) which are exactly the opposite of what we want. In order to lure people in to the CFD trap, most offer very low discount brokerage rates on share trades. Stay well clear of these companies.

Although the main things we are looking for in an online broker are low brokerage rates and no monthly fee, we do not want to compromise on safety. In every stock market collapse and financial crisis, some stockbrokers get into trouble — and a couple collapsed in the recent global financial crisis, even in Australia. There is only a small chance of this happening to your stockbroker service, but it does happen. If it is operated by one of the well-known, licenced Australian banks, we can be almost certain that they will give in to public and political pressure to ensure no individual investor loses money in the event of a collapse of their stockbroker service. This is our children's financial futures we are talking about here, so it is not worth taking the risk with CFD providers, investment banks or tiny brokerages who have no reputation to protect.

Most of the bank-owned broker services charge brokerage rates of around $20 to $30 for occasional trades (they charge less for frequent trades but our kids are not going to be trading several times per month). It is not worth taking the extra risk by using CFD providers who might charge $5 or $10 for share trades.

Almost all online broker services also offer their own in-house cash account that can be opened at the same time as the broker account. Some broker accounts can only link to their own internal cash accounts, while others also link to any other cash account operated by Australian banks, which is very handy if their in-house cash account offers lousy interest rates — which some do. Some of the smaller independent broker services don't offer their own internal cash accounts, so you need to settle each trade by sending the money (using internet banking) each time you want to buy a parcel of shares. This is not convenient. It is much better to have a specific bank account for the child that collects cash from your regular salary deductions and links automatically to the broker account.

3.8 Cash accounts

Before looking at what online broker accounts are available, we will first look at cash accounts because they go hand in hand with the broker account. Using the online broker's in-house linked cash account is the simplest solution, and they are usually opened in the same process.

However, usually the broker's in-house cash accounts don't offer the best interest rates (many are embarrassingly low), and some also have minimum balance requirement, so it is often better to opt for a different cash account offered by another bank and then link it to the broker account (if the broker account can link to other bank accounts).

Whether you are looking at the broker's in-house cash account or a separate cash account, there are several things we need for it to be ideal with our $1 per day plans.

What to look for in a cash account

A cash account is simply a bank account in which we can store cash. This account will be the place where all the contributions go, and where all the interest, dividends and other investment income is paid. About once or twice each year, the cash collected in the cash account will be used to make investments through the online broker account. Even though the total value of the investments will grow to over $1 million, there will generally only be a few thousand dollars sitting in the cash account. The rest of the money will be put to work by being invested in 'growth' investments such as shares. In the first 10 to 20 years of the simple $1 dollar per day plan, there will generally be less than $1000 sitting in the cash account. So a cash account that can be opened with a very small amount of money and pays a good rate of interest on the whole balance is needed.

A particular type of cash account that has a number of features is needed for the kids' investment plans. Your existing bank may not have accounts that are suitable, but it is a good place to start.

Only ever deal with licenced Australian banks for the kids' cash accounts. Shifty operators sometimes come up with fancy-sounding investments that have the word 'bank' in their name but they are quickly closed down by government regulators. Stick with legitimate banks you know and trust. (Did I just say trust a bank?) Well, at least they've been around for a long time, and because they are licenced by the government, we can be reasonably confident that the government will ensure that ordinary Australians don't lose their money if the bank gets into trouble (as they did in many countries during the recent global financial crisis).

Here are the tests that cash accounts need to pass in order for them to work with our plan, whether you are using the broker's internal cash account or you are linking to another cash account. The account should:

→ pay high interest — preferably around the 'official cash rate'. You can check the official target cash rate set by the Reserve Bank of Australia at <www.rba.gov.au>. There is no law that says that banks need to pay this interest rate, but most banks have accounts that pay interest rates near the official cash rate.

→ pay the high rate of interest on the whole balance in the account, calculated on the daily balance. Many accounts have 'tiered' interest rate structures which are not ideal. For example, let's say that we have $2000 in an account that pays 2 per cent interest on balances below $1000 and 5 per cent interest on balances above $1000. Make sure that the account pays 5 per cent interest on your entire balance of $2000, not just the top $1000 above the 'tier'.

→ have no regular account-keeping fees — that is, no annual fees, no monthly fees, no fees for making deposits and no fees for making withdrawals. Some cash accounts will have fees for making cheque or ATM withdrawals, but this is okay because you should not be ordering an ATM card or chequebook — never spend the money!

→ have a direct credit facility with no minimum direct credit amount. You need to be able to pay money automatically into the account — for example, automatic payments from your salary, dividends from company shares, distributions from property trusts and so on. Almost all cash accounts offered by Australian banks allow direct credits inward. If an account only allows direct credits as a 'regular savings plan' or has a 'minimum additional investment' of $100 or so, it is probably a 'managed cash fund' that invests in cash, not an actual cash account. These types of accounts are probably not going to have many of the features you need.

→ have no minimum deposit amount (after the account has been opened). Several cash funds have a minimum deposit amount of $1000 or so, which is no good for our $1 per day plan if we are just starting with $1. Also, the dividends and distributions from the investments will be paid directly into the cash account and these will be very small amounts in the early years.

→ be able to be linked with an online stockbroker service. There are several types of accounts that cannot link to broker accounts. These include passbook accounts, term deposits, cash-managed funds and many online saver accounts, which can't be opened by themselves without also opening a linked transaction account.

→ have monthly paper statements. Most accounts have paper statements, usually every month, quarter or half year. Many accounts offer online statements, but nothing beats getting a statement in the mail so you can tick off the transactions, make notes and file them away for future reference. Kids love getting letters addressed to them in the mail and they will look forward to receiving the statements. If you prefer online statements, make sure you print these out and check off the details and keep them to do tax returns.

→ have a low minimum opening balance — this is the minimum you will need to open the account. If you are starting from scratch, you need an account with a $1 opening balance. But remember, the more you start with, the bigger the fund will grow.

→ have online bank access. Almost all banks have online banking systems that allow us to view balances and transactions. This is very useful if the broker account is not able to show the cash account balance via their system.

→ have the ability to be operated by itself, without having to open another account with the same bank. There are some great-looking online saving accounts on the market that seem perfect for our needs — high interest rates, no minimum balance, no fees, etc. The only problem is that they are only allowed to be opened if you also have another expensive transaction account linked to it. This gets messy because you need to have two accounts and two statements, and you have to shuffle e-money across when you buy investments or receive dividends.

This list of tests is asking a lot of a cash account, so it is very hard to find accounts that have all these features. You can't compromise on the majority of them simply because it will not work for the $1 per day plan. The only items you may need to compromise on are:

→   online bank access. Useful, but not really necessary if you receive paper regular statements. I have had cash accounts with Adelaide Bank for years, but have never used its online banking service.

→   low minimum opening balance. You may need to compromise here because there simply are not many cash accounts that have all the required features. Generally the accounts that pay the best interest rates require a minimum opening balance of $1000 or $5000.

Features the cash account does not need are:

→   ATM or EFTPOS access. You don't want to be able to access the money at ATMs or EFTPOS terminals because you and your kids are never going to spend it!

→   a chequebook. You're never going to spend the money, so you don't need cheque access. Don't be tempted to say, 'I'll get a chequebook, just in case'. This is not an emergency cash fund for you, or a savings fund for specific purchases — this is an investment that's never going to be cashed in or spent.

→   branch access. You don't need branches because conducting transactions through them costs money and that means they will charge fees and pay lower interest rates on your money. The best cash accounts are offered by banks without big branch networks, which is how they keep the fees down and the interest rates up.

Special kids' accounts with 'bonus' interest

Many banks also offer special kids' accounts that have no monthly fees, no minimum opening or ongoing balance requirements, and pass all the other tests. They all have similar rules regarding how interest is paid. The accounts pay very low interest rates (0.1 per cent to 0.5 per cent) but they also pay what most banks call 'bonus' interest if certain conditions are met. The 'bonus' interest is paid only if there is at least one deposit in the account each month, and no withdrawals in that month. When the kids buy investments through the online broker account, these will count as 'withdrawals' from the cash account, so they will get virtually no interest for that month, which is not brilliant. Basically the kids will miss out on interest in those one or two months of each year when they buy investments, but despite their relatively low interest rates they are not a bad option for our plan, especially if it is with your main bank. The main problem is that most of these bonus interest accounts for kids are not able to be linked to online broker accounts, but they are ideal accounts for teaching the kids how to save money for shorter term goals.

Building societies and credit unions

You might also find that your local building society or credit union has the type of account you need. Many of them have good accounts and interest rates. Although it is unlikely that we would lose our money if it were deposited in a building society or credit union, I prefer to have my kids' money in a licenced bank. I've seen a couple of building societies collapse in the last big recession (Pyramid Building Society and Country-Wide Building Society in Victoria collapsed in 1990), but this is not to say that yours will too. Some have been around for over a century and will probably be here for another century. Building societies and credit unions tend to be a lot smaller and their risks tend to be a lot more concentrated than the large diverse banks. However, if you feel comfortable with your building society or credit union, give them a try, but make sure their accounts pass all of our tests.

Honeymoon rates

Some accounts offered by banks and other financial institutions have a high rate in the first six months or year, which is known as the 'honeymoon' rate, then the rate decreases. The financial institutions are hoping to attract us with a very high rate at the start, and they are also hoping that we are too lazy to change after the rate drops. Ignore the honeymoon rate and look at the ongoing rate. If that is good, and everything else stacks up, go ahead with that account. Some people actually chase the honeymoon rates all the time by opening and closing accounts every six months or so. This sounds like too much work to me. Plus it's time consuming to undo and redo all the salary deductions and dividend direct credits that need to be set up on the account. It's much easier (and probably cheaper in the long run) to pick a bank you can rely on to offer good rates and good service — and stick to it.

What about other products with higher interest rates?

In addition to the bank cash accounts, there are many investments available that appear to pay higher interest rates including:

→ enhanced cash funds bonds

→ debentures

→ fixed interest high yield securities

→ interest rate securities

→ convertible notes

→ unsecured notes

→ secured notes

→ mortgage funds

→ hybrids.

These types of securities may pay interest rates well above the cash rate, but they carry higher risks and they aren't useful for long-term investing because they don't offer any inflation protection or any prospect of growth. For the cash account, stick to cash accounts operated by a licenced bank.

But aren't we aiming to get returns of over 10 per cent per year in our plan?

Yes, we are aiming to get high returns, but we're going to do it by investing in growth assets — mainly shares. Most of the return from these assets comes in the form of capital growth, not income. Steer clear of investments that promise to pay high income because they will not work with the plan. Income investments don't provide the capital growth we need and they are generally not as tax effective. These topics are covered in more depth in chapter 4.

3.9 Online brokers & in-house cash account combinations

Now that we have covered what we need to look for in a broker account and cash account for our $1 per day plans, it's time to look at what is on the market. What we want is a good online broker account with low brokerage rates (around $20 per trade) with no regular fees, plus a good linked cash account that has no minimum balance, pays high interest on every dollar (around 5 per cent ideally) and no fees.

Even though we are starting out very small, it is possible to find pretty good combinations of broker accounts and cash accounts that will work for our plan. Terms and conditions of accounts often change, so it pays to check the latest details of each institution.

There are two ways to set up a combination that works:

→   In-house combination. This is where the broker account and cash account are offered by the same financial institution. This is the easiest and most convenient solution, but interest rates are not the best.

→   Mix and match a broker account and cash account from different financial institutions. In order to get low brokerage rates and higher interest rates on the cash account, this is often the way to go.

In-house combinations

These are simplest because they are designed to work together and are opened at the same time. Even though the interest rates on the cash accounts are not the best in the market, they have the convenience of being able to see the cash balance on the broker account screen.

The interest rates will change from time to time, but you can get a feel for whether they pay a decent rate by bearing in mind that the current official rate at the time of writing this edition is 4.75 per cent. The brokerage rates quoted below are for small trades for a few thousand dollars. All brokers charge around 0.1 per cent of the value of the trade for trades over $10 000 or so, which is cheaper than the rate for small trades, but our kids' funds will be buying small amounts for the first several years. Most broker services also offer cheaper brokerage on frequent trades (several trades per month) but we will only be doing a couple per year.

→ CommSec (owned by Commonwealth Bank)
   ph: 13 15 19
   CommSec is by far the largest online broker service in Australia. The brokerage rate is $19.95 per trade (for small trades) if using their in-house linked cash accounts. For cash accounts, they have two in-house options: their CDIA account that pays no interest under $5000, or a combination of a transaction account that is linked to the broker account (but pays no interest below $5000). The transaction account in turn is linked to an investment account that pays 5.5 per cent on every dollar. This means you need to shift money from the investment account to the transaction account before you buy shares. This combination is messier at first, but it's the best way to get $19.95 brokerage plus a good interest rate on the cash account on every dollar. The trick is to resist the temptation to use the transaction account to spend the money instead of investing it!

→ Suncorp Share Trade (owned by Suncorp Bank)
   ph: 1300 156 299
   Suncorp has a $21.95 brokerage rate. Their in-house linked cash account pays only 2.5 per cent for balances

below $20 000, with no minimum balance, but the broker account can link to cash accounts at other banks to get better interest rates.

→ NAB Online Trading (owned by National Australia Bank) <http://trading.nab.com.au/> ph: 13 13 80
NAB has a $29.95 brokerage rate. The in-house linked NAB Cash Manager account pays 4.25 per cent on every dollar. There is a minimum opening balance of $5000 but no minimum ongoing balance, so you can start with $5000 then buy shares straightaway and keep a lower cash balance. The broker account can't link to other bank accounts, but their in-house cash account is fine if you can start with $5000.

→ Westpac Online investing (Westpac Bank) <https://onlineinvesting.westpac.com.au/> ph: 13 13 31
Brokerage is $24.95 if using their in-house linked cash account, or $29.95 if linked to any other cash account for another bank. To get the lower brokerage you need to use the in-house Cash Manager account which pays virtually no interest below $5000, so it is better to link to a cash account from another bank.

→ St.George directshares (owned by Westpac) <https://invest.directshares.com.au//> ph: 13 33 30
St.George has a $32.95 brokerage rate. Linking it to the in-house Power Saver cash account pays 3.4 per cent up to $5000, which is passable, but not ideal. The broker account can also link to BankSA accounts, but not to accounts at other banks.

→ Macquarie Bank <www.macquarie.com.au/mgl/au/ personal/trading/> ph: 1800 610 924
Macquarie is set up mainly for large accounts. Their 'Edge Regular' service has $28.95 brokerage. The linked cash account has a tiered interest rate structure and very

low interest rates, but it can link to other bank accounts to get better interest rates.

→ Bell Direct (owned by Bell Potter, a full-service broker) <www.belldirect.com.au//> ph: 1300 786 199
Although Bell Direct is not owned by a bank, Bell Potter is a large, respected stockbroker and its Bell Direct service is a good low-cost online broker account. Brokerage is only $15 per trade. The linked in-house cash account pays 4 per cent with no minimum balance, and the broker account can also link to accounts at other banks.

→ E*TRADE (owned by ANZ Bank) <https://invest.etrade. com.au/Home.aspx?> ph: 1300 658 355
Brokerage is $19.95 for trades up to $5000. The in-house linked cash account pays very low rates in a tiered structure, and it can't link to accounts at other banks, so it is not good for our plan.

These are the services operated by the main players in Australia. Details change from time to time, so it pays to shop around and do a bit of research. In addition, there are many other low-cost online broker services that are run either by the CFD platform providers or by small independent operators that have come on the scene only recently. In the case of our kids' plans, we stick to the more established players. When it comes to our kids' financial futures, it is not worth chasing lower brokerage rates or higher interest rates by taking on additional risks.

Mix-and-match combinations

The second way to set up the account combination is using one of the broker accounts that can link to accounts at other banks (see previous section), and then choose a better cash account at the bank of your choice. All banks in Australia offer good cash accounts that pay high interest rates on every dollar (with no 'tiers'), no minimum balances and no monthly fees. Many of these high interest rate online cash accounts can be linked to the broker accounts I mentioned, but many cannot. Make sure you check with the bank and the broker service that the particular bank account can link to the broker account.

As the fund grows in size

As the fund grows in size, or if you can kick off the fund with $5000 initially, you will find that more options become available because cash accounts with higher minimum balance requirements also tend to pay better rates of interest. Many banks offer investment cash accounts that pay higher rates if the minimum balance is around $5000.

It is worth checking out the websites listed at the back of this book for accounts that pay higher rates of interest. Ring the bank that offers the cash account and also ring your online broker service and ask them both if the cash account can link to the broker account.

Before opening any accounts (whether they are attached to a broker service or a stand-alone cash account), always ring the broker or bank to double check that they haven't suddenly changed their terms and conditions or added a new fee. You should also always read the product disclosure statement (PDS) that comes with the product (and is also available online). This will itemise any fees and explains all the terms and conditions.

Also make sure you check out one or more of the free online services that compare different financial products including online brokers and bank accounts:

→ Infochoice: <www.infochoice.com.au>

→ Canstar: <www.http://www.canstar.com.au/>

→ Choice:

3.10 Opening the broker and cash account

Once you have selected your broker account and cash account combination and rung to double-check that the accounts will do exactly what you want them to do, it is time to open the accounts — which is the hardest part of the whole plan.

The first step is to choose the account name. Once this is decided, it is extremely important to stick to it for all other accounts and documents relating to the child's investments. This includes the use of capitals, full stops and spaces between words, brackets and so on. Changing names on accounts to fix mistakes can take a great deal of time and paperwork later on.

To open an account you will need to provide what's called a '100-point identification check', which usually means you need to provide your passport or birth certificate and a driver's licence. The accounts will be in the name of the parent(s) or grandparent(s) 'in trust for' the child. For the purpose of opening accounts, the bank will regard the parent (not the child) as the person who needs to prove identity with the 100-point check, so identification needs to be provided for the adult(s) on the account, not the child. If you already have accounts at that bank, the 100-point check may not be required for new accounts. You will generally also be asked for a tax file number. If you haven't organised the child's TFN yet, your TFN as parent and trustee for the account will generally do.

Complete the forms and send them off with a cheque for the opening deposit. After the paperwork has been sent, the broker and/or bank generally sends a letter with brochures and instructions about how the account works, as well as account numbers and passwords. An opening bank statement showing the amount used to open the account should also be sent. Congratulations — your child has their first bank statement!

Be sure to check that all details are correct, particularly the spelling of names.

When you receive the account number for the new cash account, immediately arrange for a salary deduction or direct debit from your bank account into the new account. On some accounts, this can be done in the application forms for opening the account. If you put it off, you may forget to do this and the kids' accounts will miss out on some vital contributions. You'll need that first statement when applying for a tax file number for the child. Do that straightaway too, so it's out of the way forever.

If you are setting up a separate bank account rather than the broker's in-house cash account, make sure you ring the broker service and confirm that the new cash account is actually linked to the broker account, as well as the BSB and account number. If you have opened the broker's recommended in-house cash account, their website may automatically show the cash account balance. It will be under 'portfolio balance', 'portfolio summary' or similar.

You should also spend some time familiarising yourself with the broker's website. Try looking up some companies' share prices, research, charts and so on. Most of these websites have good online tutorials and articles on many other useful subjects.

If the same broker service can be used for all the accounts in the family, they can often be linked to a single 'customer ID' so you can log on to the accounts with one password. This is fine while the kids are not involved in the plan. Once they are, though, they should be given a separate customer ID for their accounts. We don't necessarily want the kids to see all our other investments. (If they can, they may show their friends and then the whole neighbourhood would know!) It's probably a good idea to link all the kids' accounts to a single customer ID so both parents and kids can access all the kids' accounts together, while your own investments have a separate customer ID.

3.11 Bank statements

Once the kids' cash accounts have been opened, we will receive regular statements, usually each month — either in the mail or online. Once we start to hand over responsibility for the investment plan to the kids, they should be keen to get involved and check their statements. After all, it's their money and the statement will be addressed to them! If you already have kids, you will know how excited they get whenever they receive anything in the mail. (We adults don't get so excited — most of them are bills!)

The kids can check the following details on all statements:

→   opening balance — it should be the same as the closing balance on the last statement.

→   deposits from salary deductions or direct debits from parents' bank account

→   purchases or sales of investments

→   dividends and other distributions from the investments. Whenever a company or fund pays a dividend or distribution, it will send a notice in the mail advising that the payment is being made and that it will be paid directly to the cash account. Make sure that the payment notification matches the bank statement. Sometimes dividends go missing and you'll need to track them down by contacting the company that made the payment.

→ interest earned on the cash account. This will usually be paid monthly and credited to the cash account. The kids can try to check that the interest is correct.

→ closing balance. It's a good exercise for the kids to start with the opening balance, then add and subtract all the entries on the statement to arrive at the closing balance.

The kids will quickly start to get a feel for the money going in and out of their cash account. They really get excited to see investment income being paid to them on their investments. I'll never forget the first time my daughter received her first dividend — she was amazed that she got this income 'for doing nothing', and it was much more than the pocket money she made from doing chores. She soon learned that the aim is to build investments that generate investment income on their own — it's a lot easier than having to work for income!

The cash account statement will be a regular reminder of the power of investing. The value of investments in the kids' funds might go up and down each month, but the cash account will always show interest earned, so it will always be a motivating force. As soon as they see that they've earned even $10 in interest for the month they will think about how hard they had to work for that same amount by doing chores or jobs and will soon figure out that $10 in investment income is a lot easier to earn than $10 from chores.

$$$

Opening the broker account, the cash account and setting up the salary deduction are by far hardest steps in the whole plan, with the most paperwork. If you can do this, you should have few problems with the rest of the plan. Congratulations — you're on your way to building long-term wealth for your child!

Chapter 4

Investment basics

4.1 Ready to invest

So far you will have put in place the first three basic building blocks of the $1 per day plan:

1   a cash account

2   a salary deduction (or direct debit) to put cash regularly into the cash account

3   an online broker account used to buy and sell investments — linked to the cash account.

Making the commitment to the kids and actually setting up these three building blocks are the hardest parts of the plan; the rest is much easier. And now that the plan is set up, it's time to get it underway. Investing and growing the fund can be as straightforward or as complex as you want it to be. There are some very simple and effective ways to invest the money over the long term. You can stick to the simple investment approach for as long as you like, or you can add different types of investments over time as the fund grows in size and as your experience and confidence grow.

Don't forget, this is a very long-term plan. As parents, we will be in charge until the kids reach around 10 years of age, when they will start to get involved in the process. The first 10 years give us plenty of time to learn the ropes so we're ready to teach the kids when the time is right. If the kids' funds are starting out with just the $1 per day, then the cash account is a good place to keep collecting the salary deductions or direct debits for the time being. It will probably be a year or so, until the fund has grown to around $500 to $1000, before you can start investing. So we have plenty of time to start learning about the whole investment process.

There are a few concepts that you will come across all the time in your investment journey. I have tried to cover them in a way that makes them easy to introduce to the kids once they start to get involved in the plan. The issues dealt with in this chapter are:

→ inflation

→ tax

→ capital growth and income

→ investment returns

→ compounding

→ risk.

Once these have been discussed, I will look at the various types of investments for the kids' funds.

Here comes the maths

I will also begin introducing the maths involved in the plan. You don't need to do the maths if you really don't want to. But there are several good reasons why you should at least try to get a handle on some of the basic principles:

→   By working through a couple of examples in the chapters, you and your kids will have a much better understanding of how investments actually work. For example, we all know that inflation eats into the value of money, but it's not until you actually do a couple of exercises that you realise how important it is when thinking about investments. I've said that $1 per day can be turned into $1 million — but does it actually work? The examples will show your kids how to prove for themselves that it works. When they've done the maths for themselves, they will truly believe that the plan works.

→   The aim of the plan is not just to give the kids money. It is also to teach your kids how to be financially smart. The best way to do this is to lead by example. If you skip the parts explaining how investments work, how are you going to convince your kids to learn about this?

→   Over the next few years, as you put the plan into effect, you will come across all sorts of 'experts' who will try to put you off and get the money from your kids' funds into their own pocket. They will do this by telling you all sorts of myths about inflation, taxes, rates of return and many other things. Therefore, it's important to understand the basics in order to spot the con artists.

→   By understanding some of the principles, you will be in a much better position to talk to the real professionals you will come across, including your tax agents and your accountants.

→ It will also help when you read about investments in newspapers and magazines.

Next I'm going to introduce the basics, because that's where the kids will start when they begin to get involved in the plan.

4.2 Inflation

Inflation has been part of economic life since people first started living in societies and using money. In the simplest terms, inflation refers to 'price creep' — the situation when many everyday items, like housing and food, become more expensive year after year. But not everything goes up in price in this way. Some things become cheaper over time. For example, computers, televisions, digital cameras, mobile phones, MP3 players and so on all get better and better each year while they become cheaper and cheaper. On the other hand, the cost of some items, such as health insurance premiums, medical expenses, school fees and child care, often increases by much more than the average inflation rate.

One of the primary aims of government policy is to keep inflation low and prices stable. In Australia, inflation has averaged 4 per cent per year since 1900, 5.4 per cent per year since the end of the Second World War and 4.3 per cent per year since 1980. Inflation in the price of consumer items (as measured by the Consumer Price Index, which measures the prices of a basket of household expense items) ran at 2.3 per cent per year in the 1990s and has run at 3.2 per cent in the 2000s so far. The Reserve Bank of Australia's target is to keep the consumer price inflation rate to between 2 and 3 per cent per year.

An inflation rate of 3 per cent per year doesn't sound serious, but it has devastating effects on the real purchasing power of your money over time. At just 3 per cent inflation, $100 today loses 3 per cent of its real value after one year, which doesn't sound too bad, but its real value (or real purchasing power) is down to $74 after 10 years, to $55 after 20 years and to only $41 after 30 years.

The kids can easily do the maths using a calculator or spreadsheet. The real value of $100 after 20 years of inflation at 3 per cent per year = $100 ÷ (1+3%) ^ 20 = $55.37.

Since we are going to be investing over the long term, it is critical that our invesments grow in value to at least beat the inflation rate over time, and that means investing in growth assets.

So how do we stop our money from losing its real value in the future? The answer is to invest in assets that will provide a return greater than the inflation rate each year. Sometimes the inflation rate gets very high — for example, over 10 per cent per year. This occurred in Australia in the early 1920s, the early 1950s and again in the 1970s, when oil prices were rising rapidly and wages were out of control. At other times the inflation rate falls to near zero and sometimes below zero. This can happen in recessions, when unemployment rises, businesses close down and the economy stops growing. This happened in Australia in the early 1980s and again in the early 1990s.

It is, therefore, important to understand how inflation affects different types of investments. Some types will grow in value to keep us ahead of inflation, but others will not. We also need to plan to have our investments 'beat' inflation by a good margin, because there is no guarantee that the inflation rate will not start to rise again in the years ahead.

In our kids' investment funds we will be investing in growth assets (shares and property), which are expected to grow faster than the inflation rate over the long term. It is also important that we increase our regular contributions to the funds each year, when we can, in order to keep ahead of inflation.

4.3 Tax

Most people hate paying tax. In Australia, almost everybody and everything is taxed. There are hundreds of different types of taxes. What I am going to look at here is income tax. However, this section is not intended as comprehensive tax advice, it simply outlines some of the current rules. You should always check the latest details at <www.ato.gov.au> and talk to your accountant about your specific circumstances.

Generally, all income from investments is taxable, but the capital growth of the investments is generally not taxed unless and until the asset is sold, which may be many years or decades away.

Different types of investments are taxed in different ways. For example, in the case of bank accounts, there is no capital growth, but the investment return is in the form of interest income, which is taxable income. In the case of 'growth' assets such as shares and many types of property, on the other hand, most of the total investment return is in the form of capital growth (which is generally not taxable unless it is sold), while the income return is usually lower (so the tax is lower).

Money in the bank is safe and secure, but it is not a good long-term investment because money in the bank goes backwards after taxes and after inflation. Bank accounts are useful places to store money while we're planning to put it to better use by investing it. They are also useful for storing money in case we need it for emergencies. We need to put our money into different types of investments in order to make them earn a lot more than the inflation rate after tax. The aim is to make our money grow, not shrink in value due to the impact of taxes and inflation.

4.4 Capital and income

One of the most difficult concepts to explain to kids is the difference between capital and income, and therefore the difference between capital growth and income. For example, what does 'living off the income from investments but never spending the capital' actually mean? If you buy $1000 worth of BHP shares today, they might be worth $1050 after one year, so the capital growth is $50. During the same year those BHP shares might also produce 'income' of $50 in dividends. If, on the other hand, you start the year with $1000 in a cash account paying interest of 5 per cent and by the end of the year the balance has increased to $1050, is that extra $50 'capital growth' or is it 'income', and does it really matter?

Understanding the difference between capital and income is important because we will come across these terms constantly as we grow the investment fund.

Apple trees and apples

Think about an investment as an apple tree. Let's assume that some types of apple trees grow and some stay the same size. Also, some types of apple trees produce apples each year and others don't. We can think about different types of investments as different types of apple trees.

Let's say Investor A has $100 and puts it in a bank account that pays interest at 5 per cent per year, paid at the end of each year. I will call the original $100 'capital'. One year later there will be $105 in the account, but only $100 of that is capital. It stays in the bank account and never grows to be worth more than $100. But that $100 capital will generate 'income', in the form of interest at a rate of 5 per cent per year. The original $100 has not grown in value; it is the same $100 that Investor A put in originally. The extra $5 in the account is income. Therefore, the $105 in the account at the end of the year consists of $100 in capital plus $5 in income.

Investor B also started with $100 in capital and, instead of putting it in the bank, bought gold bullion. (Investors can buy gold bullion, which is 99.99 per cent pure gold made into gold bars.) For the purpose of this example, let's assume that gold goes up in value by 5 per cent per year. On the first day of the year Investor B bought gold bullion worth $100. At the end of the year, gold had increased 5 per cent over the year, so Investor B's gold is now worth $105.

In the example above Investors A and B both started the year with capital of $100, and they both ended the year with $105. So what's the difference and does it really matter?

Investor A's $100 in a bank account is like 100 apple trees (capital) that always stay the same size. At the end of the year there are still 100 apple trees (their capital was exactly the same size), but those 100 apple trees have produced a total of 5 apples (income). Because interest income is taxable, the investor will need to pay tax on the income.

On the other hand, Investor B's $100 investment in gold is like 100 apple trees that have grown in size. There are still 100 apple trees but each tree is 5 per cent bigger. The capital has grown from $100 to $105 over the year. The trees produced no apples (no income), but they grew bigger (produced capital growth of $5).

Tax on capital and income

The first difference between income and capital growth is tax. Investors are taxed on income when it is earned or when it is received. Investor A will need to pay income tax on the $5 of income at the end of the year and will have to take some money out of the account to do so. If Investor A is in the 30 per cent tax bracket, they would pay tax of 31.5 per cent tax (30 per cent plus 1.5 per cent Medicare levy). Income tax on the interest will be $1.58 ($5 × 31.5% tax), so they will end up with $103.42 in the account ($105 less tax of $1.58).

On the other hand, Investor B received no income from the gold and therefore pays no tax. They have received capital growth from the gold, because the value has grown from $100 to $105. But capital growth is only taxed when the asset is sold, which might not be for many years, perhaps never. This is called capital gains tax (CGT).

If both investors hold their investments for several years, Investor B will be much better off (assuming the bank account keeps paying 5 per cent interest and the value of gold keeps growing at 5 per cent per year). Investor A will have to take money out of the account (or from somewhere else) every year to pay tax. But Investor B pays no tax for as long as they hold on to the gold. All the capital (the gold) is kept intact and continues to grow in value.

Tax rates

The second difference between income and capital growth is the rate of tax payable. Let's assume that both investors are in the same 30 per cent tax bracket. We have just seen that Investor A with the bank account will have to pay tax every year on the interest income earned from the investment. We also saw that Investor B with the gold doesn't pay tax at all on the capital growth from the gold unless it is sold.

Investor A will have to pay tax at their marginal tax rate. As mentioned, Investor A pays tax on interest income at 31.5 per cent. But capital gains are taxed at lower rates than interest income. If investments are held by individuals, the tax rate on capital gains is half the tax rate payable on other forms of income (like interest). (Note that assets held by other types of entities, such as companies and super funds, are treated differently, but investments held by individuals are given a 50 per cent discount on the CGT rate if the asset is held for more than one year.) Therefore, if Investor B sold the gold after 10 years, there would be a 15 per cent tax (half of 30 per cent) on the capital gain. Investor B only pays tax if they sell the asset. If Investor B does sell the asset, the tax paid is much less than Investor A pays. Investor B also gets to pay the tax at the end, when the asset is sold, rather than every year like Investor A. This is shown in table 4.1.

Table 4.1: differences between tax paid on income and tax paid on capital growth

	Income	Capital growth
Example	Bank interest	Gold bullion
Type of return	Apples	Growth in size of the apple trees
Payment of tax	Each year	Only if and when the asset is sold
Tax rate	Investor's marginal tax rate	Half the investor's marginal tax rate

Keep in mind that I used gold bullion merely as an example of a type of asset that doesn't produce income, but it doesn't always grow in value. It often falls in value as well, and that produces capital losses instead of capital gains. The value of gold goes up and down over time, so it is a 'risky' asset, whereas the value of money in the bank stays stable and constant (but it loses purchasing power over time due to the impact of inflation).

Many types of investments, such as shares, produce both capital growth (or losses) as well as income. This is like having apple trees that grow each year (capital gains) and that also produce apples (income in the form of dividends). A good share portfolio should increase in capital value over time, like trees that grow bigger each year. And companies that grow in capital value also tend to increase the dividend income they pay shareholders — as the trees grow bigger, they also tend to produce more apples each year. Shareholders pay income tax on the dividend income they receive each year, but don't pay tax on the capital gains unless and until they sell the shares.

Living off capital versus living off income

In chapter 1 I talked about people living off investment capital, as opposed to living off investment income. It is important to understand the difference between the two. Let's say you have $1 million in investment capital. This investment capital might produce investment income of 5 per cent per year. The investment income, therefore, is $50 000 per year ($1 million × 5%).

Assuming you had no other sources of income, and that your living expenses were $50 000 per year, you would be able to live off the investment income of $50 000 and wouldn't need to sell part of the investment capital to pay for your living expenses. Think of the investment assets as one million apple trees. These trees produce 50 000 apples per year, which is enough for you to live on, so it's not necessary to cut down any of the trees to sell the wood to cover your expenses each year. This way you are keeping your trees (capital) intact for the future.

On the other hand, if your living expenses were $80 000 per year, which is greater than your income ($50 000), you would have to sell $30 000 worth of assets in order to pay for your expenses each year. You would be eating into your capital. This is like one million apple trees that produce 50 000 apples per year, which is not enough to survive on, so 30 000 trees (part of our capital) need to be cut down and the wood sold in order to cover the shortfall of $30 000 each year.

If you cut down trees each year to cover living expenses, two things would happen. First, you would have fewer trees each year, so the number of apples produced (income) would be lower. Second, you would eventually run out of trees (capital), so no investment income would be produced.

The aim of this plan is to grow investment assets for your kids so that they produce enough investment income to pay for all your living expenses, so you don't have to start eating into capital.

The capital needs to be kept intact so it continues to grow over time and produce more and more income each year, to keep ahead of inflation.

The income our family lives off is generated from shares, some of which I have owned for 20 years. The capital gains over that time have been completely tax free, and the dividend income has grown well in excess of the inflation rate. We will probably never sell the shares, so we will probably never pay capital gains tax on them. If we did decide to sell some, we would do it in years in which other income is low, so we minimise or eliminate capital gains tax.

4.5 Investment returns

When I look at various types of investments, I will examine the types of returns that can be expected from them. The return can be in the form of capital growth and/or income.

It's necessary to know how these returns are taxed so the after-tax return we can expect from that type of investment can be estimated. We will need to look at the after-tax return to make sure that the investment will keep ahead of inflation over the long term and that it will get us to $1 million.

When looking at the returns from a particular investment we need to look at the total return — that is, from both capital growth and income. If we hear that the return from the sharemarket in a particular year was 10 per cent, this is likely to consist of around 6 per cent capital growth plus around 4 per cent dividend income. Similarly, a commercial building might also produce a total return of 10 per cent for the year. But, in the case of the building, it is more likely to consist of rent at maybe 7 per cent per year plus capital growth in the value of the building of 3 per cent. Each type of investment will have a different proportion of capital growth and income in its total return for the year, and this break-up of growth and income will also tend to change from year to year.

Total return or return per year

Let's say you bought investment XYZ for $100 and sold it for $200 five years later. That looks like a pretty good return. That's a 100 per cent gain over five years. If you bought another investment, UVW, for $100 and sold it 10 years later for $200, that has also returned 100 per cent, but it took 10 years.

Which investment has provided the better return — XYZ or UVW (assuming they carried the same risk)? They both returned 100 per cent on our investment of $100. But which would you rather own? The answer is XYZ, because the same 100 per cent return was generated in only five years.

When measuring and comparing investment returns we need to take all returns back to a common base — we need to look at return per year or per annum. Investment XYZ must have produced a higher average return per year than investment UVW, because it reached $200 five years sooner than investment UVW. What would you guess that rate of return is for XYZ? Around 20 per cent?

Calculating returns per year

When calculating the return per year, the effect of compounding needs to be included. A financial calculator or spreadsheet is required to work out what the return or growth rate is per year. For example, if investment XYZ grew from $100 to $200 over five years, the return per year is calculated in the following way:

> = ($200 ÷ $100) to the power of (1 ÷ the number of years) – 1
>
> = ($200 ÷ $100) ^ (1 ÷ 5) – 1
>
> = 14.9%

The return per year can be double-checked with a basic calculator:

> = $100 × 114.9% × 114.9% × 114.9% × 114.9% × 114.9%
>
> = $200

Or:

> = $100 × 1.149 × 1.149 × 1.149 × 1.149 × 1.149
>
> = $200

Or, using a financial calculator with a 'to the power of' function or spreadsheet:

> = $100 multiplied by (1 + 14.9%) to the power of 5
>
> = $100 × (1 + 14.9%) ^ 5
>
> = $200

The average annual rate of return or growth has been 14.9 per cent per year, which is somewhat below our 'guess' of 20 per cent. This is because the return has compounded each year. The annual growth rate is sometimes called the compound annual growth rate (CAGR). This term often appears in company reports, prospectuses and product disclosure statements (PDSs), which provide information about investments.

Investment UVW also doubled from $100 to $200 but took 10 years to do this. The average annual return for investment UVW is only 7.2 per cent when calculated in the same way as the above example.

When the total return of 100 per cent over the full period is converted to an annual return per year, it is easy to see which investment produced the higher return per year. Investment XYZ returned 14.9 per cent per year, which is more than double the return per year of investment UVW, at 7.2 per cent per year.

Fortunately, we don't have to do the maths very often. Throughout the investment world, rates of return and growth are usually converted to annual returns, the CAGR. For example, a research report on a particular company might talk about a dividend rate being 3.5 per cent, or a growth rate being 12 per cent. These almost always refer to annual rates. I say 'almost always' because we will sometimes come across shonky operators who try to mislead us. For example, an advertisement for a particular type of investment might promise '50 per cent returns!'. But the fine print might say that this return is over a period of 10 years. And a 50 per cent return over 10 years is only around 4 per cent compound annual return per year, which is not that flash — especially since it's probably high-risk as well.

4.6 Compounding

It's now time to take a look at compounding — how it works and why it's an important part of our investment plan. I said in chapter 1 that an investment fund of $1 million can be grown by putting in $1 per day for 50 years. In the simplest plan you can start with just $1, contribute $31 per month and increase the contributions by 3 per cent each year to stay ahead of inflation.

Under this version of the plan the total amount the parents and the child put in over the 50 years would be $53 390 (or around $25 000 in today's dollars assuming inflation of 2.5 per cent over the next 50 years). So how can these contributions of $53 000 somehow turn into $1 million? Part of the answer is that we invest the money primarily in Australian shares, and these can produce average returns of around 11 per cent per year. (I will cover returns expected from shares in detail in chapters 5 and 6.)

But even if we put in the entire $53 000 on day 1 and invested it at 11 per cent for the whole 50-year period, that would amount to total investment earnings of $291 000 ($53 000 × 11% investment earnings per year = $5830 earnings each year × 50 years).

This is nowhere near the $1 million total value of the fund, so where does the rest of the money come from?

Reinvesting all investment earnings

In our kids' investment funds, we reinvest all the investment earnings from the fund so the fund total will grow faster each year. We do this because the kids don't need the earnings to live on. When the kids start contributing to their fund, they will only be putting part of their pocket money and part of any other income (from gifts and part-time jobs) into the fund. They will still have money for 'savings' and 'spending'. By reinvesting all of the fund earnings, the fund will reach $1 million in time for them to enjoy it when they are 40 or 50 years old.

In practical terms, reinvesting the investment earnings is easy to arrange. For the money sitting in the cash account, the interest is automatically paid into that account. Whenever we buy an investment using money in the cash account, we will be sent a form in which we can request that all dividends, distributions and other investment income be credited to the cash account. We're now reinvesting the fund earnings back into the fund and we're on track for the $1 million.

Therefore, the lesson is don't take the income out of the fund and spend it or put it under the bed. Plant those seeds and grow more trees — reinvest all the investment earnings back into the fund and it will grow faster each year.

One cent per day exercise

Here's an example of the power of compounding and exponential growth. Say to your kids, 'I want you to go and find 1 cent and put it into a jar today. Tomorrow put in 2 cents. On day three put in 4 cents. On day four put in 8 cents. Each day, put in twice the amount you put in the previous day. After 31 days, stop and count up all the money.'

Actually get them to put down this book and go and find a jar and a 1 cent coin. Pretty hard these days because copper coins are no longer used. But they may find a few in old money boxes or under the seat cushions. If you can't find real cents, ask them to use game tokens or make pretend coins for this exercise. (We could do this exercise starting with a dollar instead, but the numbers get too big. It's more effective if we use cents. The point is that even 'worthless' cents can add up to a big total.)

How much do you think you would end up with in a jar at the end of 31 days if you put in 1 cent on the first day and kept doubling the contributions each day for 31 days? Which of the following amounts do you think would be closest to the correct answer:

a $0.31

b $31

c $100

d $400

e $1000

Circle your answer and put a mark against your kids' answers so you can tell who guessed which answer.

For the first few days the kids will happily search around the house for loose change and put the right amount of money in the jar each day. Get them to write down the amount they put in each day and the running total of how much money is in the jar. Now, ask the kids where they would like to donate the money at the end of the 31 days. They might like to donate it to the school library or the Red Cross. Write the name of the charity at the top of the sheet of paper. After 10 days the sheet of paper should look like table 4.2.

By day 10 the kids will probably be having difficulty finding coins. And you'll be wondering where this will end up. As shown in table 4.2, after 10 days the fund balance in the jar is $10.23.

Table 4.2: amount of money collected after 10 days

Charity: Smithtown school library		
Day	Contribution $	Running total $
1	0.01	0.01
2	0.02	0.03
3	0.04	0.07
4	0.08	0.15
5	0.16	0.31
6	0.32	0.63
7	0.64	1.27
8	1.28	2.55
9	2.56	5.11
10	5.12	10.23

Well, let me tell you this — nobody has ever managed to make it to day 31 in this game. If you were able to stick to the plan, on day 31 you would have to put in — wait for it… $10737 418.24. That's right — over $10 million dollars! On day 31 the running total in the jar would be a whopping $21 474 836.47! That's a pretty big jar. I hope that promise you made to pay the school library wasn't a binding contract!

Once you and the kids realise that you're going to have to move to a bigger house to accommodate the size of the jar you'll need, you'll have to have a family meeting and unanimously agree to abandon the plan and quietly cancel the promise to make the donation to the school library! Ask the kids to draw a chart of the fund balance as it grows over the 31 days. The chart should be drawn in pencil. They will find that they have to make several attempts at it because they will get the scale on the Y-axis (the vertical line on the left side of the chart that shows the total in the jar) wrong every time. Once they've done the calculations over 31 days they will realise that the Y-axis must go up to over $21 million!

The line showing the total over the 31 days will be a curve heading upwards, getting steeper as it grows faster each day. This is compound or exponential growth.

Figure 4.1 shows what the chart would look like if a normal Y-axis is used.

Figure 4.1: 1 cent per day for 31 days using a normal Y-axis

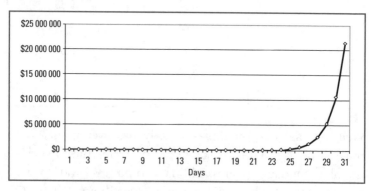

In order to see the exponential (compound) growth more clearly, a logarithmic scale for the Y-axis should be used. This can easily be done in Excel by selecting 'Logarithmic' as an option in the 'Scale' menu in 'Chart options'. If the kids are doing the chart on paper, they can easily create a logarithmic Y-axis scale by dividing the Y-axis into 10 equal sections and, starting from the bottom, labelling them: $0.01, $0.10, $1, $10, $100, $1000, $10000, $100000, $1 million, $10 million and $100 million. The labels multiply by 10 in each step. Labels that multiply are used because the investment fund also multiplies as it grows.

Figure 4.2 shows what the chart would look like if a logarithmic Y-axis is used.

Figure 4.2: 1 cent per day for 31 days using a logarithmic Y-axis

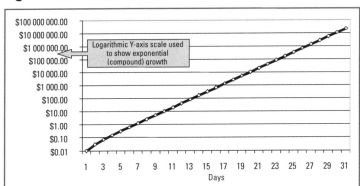

This exercise demonstrates compounding in its most extreme form. It's a powerful concept, and we are going to put it to good use by reinvesting all those earnings in our kids' investment funds. Keep up the regular $31 per month contributions, invest in growth assets and reinvest all earnings — and let compounding take care of the rest.

4.7 Prove that the $1 per day plan really works

By now the kids should have a pretty good idea of how compounding works and how tiny contributions really add up to a huge total over time. This is how the contributions of $1 per day into the kids' fund can grow into $1 million if all the earnings each year are reinvested and never spent.

The kids can now have a go at working out how the $1 per day investment plan compounds over 50 years. This is much easier to do on a computer spreadsheet, but it can be done using a basic calculator. The rules are simple in the basic plan:

→ Start with $1.

→ In the first year, add contributions of $31 at the end of each month.

→ At the end of the year, add investment returns (using 11 per cent for the long-term average expected returns).

→ Also at the end of the year, add any extra annual contributions (like birthday or Christmas contributions).

→ For the next year, increase the monthly contributions by 3 per cent (and round up to the nearest $1, so the contributions in year 2 would be $32 per month not $31.93).

→ Repeat for each year.

Get the kids to keep doing this up to, say, year 10, or as far as they want to go. They will notice that from around year 8 onward the return on the fund each year will be bigger than the contributions each year. This is an important milestone to reach. This means that, from then on, most of the fund's growth will be coming mainly from reinvestment of earnings rather than from new contributions to the fund.

They will arrive at numbers similar to those in table 1.1 in chapter 1. Figure 4.3 shows what the first 10 years of the plan should look like.

Figure 4.3 shows that the total contributions over the first 10 years are $4479, but the fund balance has grown to around $7600 because all earnings have been reinvested. (Assuming returns are 11 per cent per year, the total would be $7580, but because in real life returns always vary from year to year, the actual balance is likely to be between $6000 and $9000.) The difference between the total contributions and the fund balance is the effect of compounding. The solid black line on the chart shows the balance if the fund achieves 11 per cent returns each year, but in practice the returns will vary from year to year. The shaded area around the black line shows the range of expected outcomes as returns vary over the years.

I introduced our daughter to the plan when she was 10, and at that stage my wife and I had contributed around $4000 to her fund but it had grown to over $10 000. The other $6000 that had magically appeared was simply due to compounding. There is no magic in it at all.

Figure 4.3: $1 per day at 11 per cent return per annum— first 10 years

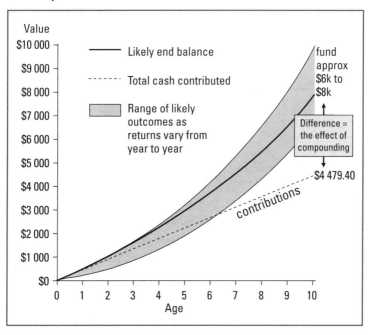

If you continued to calculate the balance for 50 years, the chart would look like figure 4.4 (overleaf). Over 50 years the power of compounding can be seen very clearly. The total of the contributions is barely above zero on the chart, but the total fund balance has shot up toward $1 million. That's the power of compounding—reinvesting all the earnings back into the fund and never spending it. If a logarithmic scale on the Y-axis is used, the chart becomes clearer, as shown in figure 4.2.

Figure 4.4: $1 per day at 11 per cent per annum for 50 years

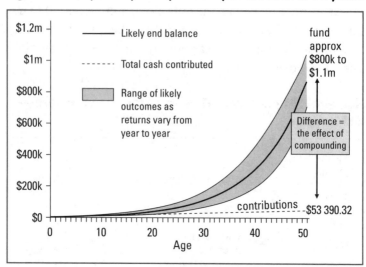

By doing the maths and creating the charts, the kids have just proved that they can reach $1 million by investing and starting out with just $1 per day. In real life the fund balance will not go up in a smooth line like in these charts. Actual returns will vary from year to year, but in the long term they will get to the target. In both of our kids' plans the balances have gone up and down over the years, but they are both still on track for the $1 million. As in figure 4.3, the solid black line in the 50-year chart shows what the fund balance would be if returns were 11 per cent each year, but since returns vary from year to year, the shaded area shows the range of likely outcomes with variable returns each year.

Repaying the loan for the parents' contributions

As I've mentioned, over the first 15 years or so, until the kids take over the responsibility for the fund and for the $1 per day contributions, the parents' contributions will total around $7500. Once the kids have regular part-time jobs, they can take over the responsibility for the $1 per day contributions and parents can stop making their contributions. When we hand over the responsibility of the fund to our kids, we will say to them, 'Our contributions were just a loan to get you started. When you turn 40 (for example), we want our loan for the contributions back.'

Take a look at the total fund balance at age 40 in table 1.1 in chapter 1, and in the charts you've just drawn. The fund balance would be about $300 000 to $350 000 after 40 years, and only about $34 000, or around 10 per cent of the fund balance, has come from contributions. The other 90 per cent, or $300 000 or so, will have come from continually reinvesting the earnings back into the fund. If your $7500 loan is repaid at that point, it will only make a very small dent in the total fund value. (The parents' contributions of around $7500 are only around 2 per cent of the fund value.) The fund will still have $320 000 or so to keep on growing. The kids will be well on the way to the $1 million target.

4.8 Main types of investments

There are two main types of investments — 'debt' investments and 'equity' investments. When I say 'debt' here, I'm not talking about credit card debt or home loan debt. For investors, the word 'debt' means that you are the lender, not the borrower. Let's see how debt and equity work.

Suppose you have young kids who want to make some money by setting up a lemonade stand in the street. They need $10 to cover the cost of lemonade and paper cups, but they only have $5 and so they ask you for the other $5. Treating this as a business venture, you have two choices. You could invest in their business as debt, in which case you would lend them $5 and tell them you want it — plus interest of, say, $1 — paid back at the end of the day. This would mean you got back $6, representing a 20 per cent return on your investment. Or you could give them the $5 as an equity partner in the venture, which means that you would be entitled to a 50:50 share of the profits. If the kids made a net profit of, say, $20, you would get back $10, representing a 100 per cent return on your investment. If, on the other hand, their net profit was only $5, you would get back $2.50, representing a 50 per cent loss on your investment.

That's it — if we invest as debt, we are lending money to the business. The business promises to pay back 100 per cent of our money plus interest, but not a share of the profits. The upside is limited (to the amount of interest payable) but so is the downside, because we are paid first, before the equity owners. On the other hand, equity owners get to share in the profits and growth of the business if it succeeds. The downside is greater because equity owners get paid only after debts are paid, but if the business is a success the upside is much greater.

Income (debt) investments

Debt investments are often called income investments because they produce income (usually interest on the debt) instead of capital growth. The simplest type of income or debt investment is depositing money in a bank account, because we are actually lending the money to the bank. The cash is 'at call' because the bank promises to repay us any time we 'call' for it.

Income (debt) investments include:

→   cash accounts with banks and other financial institutions

→ term deposits

→ bank bills

→ debentures

→ mortgage funds

→ promissory notes

→ government bonds

→ corporate bonds

→ floating rate notes.

I won't spend too much time on income (debt) investments because they are mainly for people who want regular income to live off. They are not ideal for building wealth over the long term, because the returns are only in the form of taxable income (interest) and they offer no protection against inflation and no real growth above inflation. The only income investment we will have in our kids' investment funds is money in the cash account. The cash accumulates there from our regular salary deductions or direct debits, and we keep it in that account until it builds up to an amount large enough to start investing it in growth assets.

A couple of times each year we take the money that has accumulated in the cash account and invest it in growth investments. After the first few years, this will amount to less than 5 per cent of our total investment portfolio.

Growth (equity ownership) investments

The two main types of growth investments are company shares and property. They are usually called growth assets instead of equity assets, because 'equity' has come to mean company shares only.

In the case of both company shares and property, we are buying an ownership stake in the business or property. The value of the business or property might go up or down over time, and our share in the profits (dividends in the case of companies, and rent in the case of property) might go up or down from year to year. Investing in shares and property is like investing in apple trees that grow in height (and can also shrink) over time — but, it is hoped, grow to great heights in the long term. Most of these apple trees also produce income in the form of apples (dividends and rent), but the number of apples produced might vary from year to year, or production may cease altogether.

Investors looking for long-term growth (like our kids in their investment funds) generally invest in growth assets like company shares and property. Our kids are not going to need any income from their investment funds for 40 or 50 years, so inflation protection and capital growth are far more important than income. Any income in the form of dividends and rent can be reinvested in the fund to make it grow faster.

As investors we can often choose how we want to invest in a particular business. Earlier, I used the example of my kids' lemonade stand. Another example is Woolworths. If we were looking for regular, stable income, we could invest in Woolworths Perpetual Floating Rate Notes (ASX code: WOWHB). This is a debt investment; when we buy these we are the lender and Woolworths is the borrower. Woolworths pays us a quarterly income for as long as we own the investment. The notes pay around 6 per cent to 7 per cent interest per year. (It varies, depending on the market interest rates at the time — hence the term 'floating rate'.) We don't get to share in the growth of the Woolworths business, but we do get a good income from the investment. This might be a good income investment, but it wouldn't do much in a growth portfolio — we would have to pay tax on the income each year and the capital value of the investment wouldn't grow. This is like an apple tree that produces a lot of apples each year but never grows. In 50 years' time, the apple tree will be the same height as it is today and will produce the same number of apples it produces today. So it won't even keep pace with inflation.

On the other hand, Woolworths has been a great business success, and the value of the business has grown substantially and consistently over many years. If we wanted a growth investment, we could buy shares in the company itself (WOW). When our daughter was born Woolworths shares were around $3 per share. At the time of writing, they are above $25 per share. The total returns, including share price growth plus dividends, have been more than 15 per cent per year for more than a decade and a half, even after the global financial crisis. Our family has owned shares in Woolworths and many other companies like it for many years, and we have been saying 'WOW!' ever since!

Of course, there are no guarantees that future returns will be the same as past returns, but this is an example of how investors can choose to invest in either debt or equity.

This means that if we invested in Woolworths shares we could get good capital growth but a relatively low income. This type of investment is what we will be looking for to help the kids' investment funds reach $1 million. It's like an apple tree that has grown to nearly 10 times its size over the past 15 years and has produced many more apples each year.

In the same way we can also invest in the big banks like the Commonwealth, National Australia Bank, ANZ Bank and Westpac. We could invest in a range of debt investments offered by each bank, including cash deposits, term deposits, debentures, floating rate notes and preference shares. For an income investor, these various forms of debt investments offer an income return of around 3 per cent or 4 per cent per year up to around 6 per cent to 7 per cent per year, but no protection against inflation and no growth. However, investors looking for capital growth can invest in shares in the banks themselves. Investors who bought shares in pretty much any of the banks 10 years ago would have made average returns of well over 10 per cent to 15 per cent per year since, even with the global financial crisis. Sure beats putting money in the bank!

4.9 Other types of investments

There are many other types of things that appear to be 'investments', including:

→ *Superannuation*. Superannuation is not an investment but a structure for holding investments. Our $1 per day plan is not intended to replace super. Our kids will have their own super funds when they start working, but they will probably not be able to access the money until they are 65 or 70 years old by the time the government is through fiddling with the complex rules.

→ *Managed funds*. A managed fund is not an investment but a structure for holding investments. We cover managed funds in later chapters.

→ *Insurance bonds*. These are a structured product that can hold a range of investments, but they are usually riddled with layers of fees and sales commissions.

→ *Education bonds*. Education bonds are generally built around the structure of an insurance bond, and they claim to be tax-free when we get the money back in 10 years. This is misleading because the fund has been paying tax out of our money every year for those 10 years, so it's not tax-free at all. All 'tax-free' means is that the tax has already been paid every year and that we don't pay tax again on the money when we withdraw it. Moreover, tax is paid at the rate of 30 per cent, which is a higher tax rate than our kids will be paying with their $1 per day fund.

Also, many education bonds charge extremely high fees and sales commissions, which eat into the capital. Another disadvantage is that they only let investors take their money out for their child's education. In our case we are not going to take the money out at all. When our kids are 40 or 50 years old they are going to be able to use some of the investment income and retire early or semi-retire, but leave the capital intact. Education bonds will not allow them to do this.

4.10 Investing versus trading

Investing and trading are very different activities. Investors spend time researching each investment and aim to build wealth by holding investments for long periods — five to 10 years or more. They are not concerned about what the share price is doing in the short term, and only look to sell an asset if there is something seriously wrong with the business or if the outlook for the industry in which it operates is very poor. Traders, in contrast, usually buy assets for very short periods of time — for example, day traders might buy in the morning, then buy and sell during the day, and sell all their holdings by the close of business every day. Then they do it all again the next day. Traders set out to build wealth by doing thousands of trades. Each trade might only make a few dollars' profit, but from thousands of trades over many years many traders can make a good living. Because traders are doing so many transactions, they need large amounts of capital. They are also competing against other big traders all over the world, and they can't do that with small stakes.

Don't believe the advertisements you see that say we can buy a trading 'system' for a few thousand dollars, spend 10 minutes each day trading, then spend the rest of the day sipping martinis by the pool, counting our money. The only people getting rich are the people selling the trading systems.

Part IV

GO!

Chapter 5

Company shares

5.1 Shares

It's time now to examine the primary source of growth for long-term investment funds — company shares. The terms 'shares', 'stocks' and 'equities' mean the same thing — investing in the ownership of companies and businesses. A share in a company is just a tiny piece of the ownership of a company. By owning shares in a company we become an equity partner with all the other shareholders in the company. The sharemarket, the stock market and the equities markets are different names for the same thing — the market in which people buy and sell shares in companies.

The Australian Stock Exchange

The Australian Stock Exchange (ASX) lets investors buy and sell shares in companies easily, quickly and cheaply. ('ASX' now actually stands for 'Australian Securities Exchange', but everybody still knows it as the Australian Stock Exchange.) Around 2000 companies have their shares listed on the ASX, and we can buy and sell shares in any one of them if we want to. As well as being able to buy and sell company shares on the ASX, we can buy many other types of investments — including property trusts, share trusts, preference shares, hybrids and cash funds. But the main function of the ASX is to provide a market for investors to buy and sell shares in companies.

Every company listed on the ASX has a code, which makes them easy to find. For example, the ASX code for ANZ Bank is 'ANZ'. Log onto the ASX website, type in ANZ, and you can watch people buying and selling ANZ shares all day while the market is open. Every day several million shares in ANZ change hands.

If you wanted to buy 20 shares in ANZ, you could log onto your online broker account and place a 'buy' order for 20 shares at $25 per share (if that was the current price). Once the trade is 'executed', you would own 20 shares in ANZ worth a total of around $500. The cost of buying the shares would be 'brokerage' (including GST) of around $20 charged by the online broker, so the total cost would be $520. It all takes just a few seconds and you're a shareholder almost before you know it.

The value of shares changes

Every day (and every minute of every trading day) the share price of ANZ can change. If we bought our shares at 11.00 am on Monday for $25 per share, we might look at the price (on our broker account website or on the ASX website) later that same day and see that it has gone up to $25.50 or that it has fallen to $24.00. One year later our ANZ shares might have gone up to $30.00 or they might have fallen to $20.00. If that happened, our $500 investment would be worth only $400.

There is no guarantee offered by ANZ or the ASX that we will get back the money that we put in when we bought the shares, or that we will get back any money at all. It's just like investing in equity in the lemonade stand — there are no guarantees and we could lose the lot. We have all heard about companies like One.Tel, HIH, Babcock & Brown and ABC Learning that simply went broke and ceased to exist. Their shareholders lost the lot, and so did most of the owners of the debts as well in those cases! We hope, of course, that we will be investing in companies that grow in value over time. We will also be diversifying across many companies so as to reduce risk.

5.2 Dividends

Unlike debt or income investments, companies don't pay interest to their shareholders. But most companies listed on the ASX pay their shareholders income in the form of 'dividends' on their shareholdings. These dividends are a share of the profits that the company has made from running its businesses. Dividends are usually paid every half-year. There is an interim dividend paid around halfway through the company's financial year and a final dividend paid around the end of the company's financial year.

The dividends paid by companies don't necessarily stay the same from year to year. Sometimes a company will reduce the dividends, but most of the time it will increase them as the business grows. Sometimes a company will stop paying dividends altogether. We can find out what dividends ANZ is paying by keying in the ANZ code on the ASX website or on our online broker account website, or we can look it up in the business section of newspapers, where it will appear in the 'dividends per share' column in the share listings. Your online broker website would also show the dividends paid by each company going back many years, so you can see how consistently dividends have been growing.

Franking credits

Companies pay tax on their profits from running their businesses. Let's say we owned 100 shares in XYZ company and it made a net profit before tax of $100 million in a particular year. It would pay tax at the company tax rate, which is 30 per cent at the time of writing, so XYZ would pay $30 million to the tax office, leaving a profit after tax of $70 million for the year. If there are 100 million shares on issue, the profit after tax would be 70 cents per share ($70 million profit after tax divided by 100 million shares).

What does the company do with that $70 million in profit after tax? It pays part of it to its shareholders (owners) as dividends, and it retains the rest to reinvest in the business (to buy new equipment and so on). Let's say in that year it decided to pay its shareholders 50 cents per share in dividends and retain the remaining 20 cents per share to reinvest in the business.

When we receive our dividend (either as a cheque or as direct credit to the cash account), a statement informing us of the transaction is sent, as shown in table 5.1.

Table 5.1: transaction statement

Number of shares	Dividend per share	Total dividend	% franked	Franking credit per share	Total franking credits
100	50 cents	$50.00	100	21.4286 cents	$21.43

The '% franked' in the fourth column refers to the proportion of the company's profits that was taxed at the company tax rate. In this case, 100 per cent of the profit was taxed at the company tax rate of 30 per cent. This is normal for most companies.

The fifth column shows that the franking credits per share were 21.4286 cents. If the company tax rate is 30 per cent, then the franking credit was:

= 50 cents per share dividend × 30% ÷ 70%

= 21.4286 cents per share.

Why is all this important? Because it will reduce our tax and even get us a tax refund. At the end of the year we will receive a tax credit for the amount that the company has already paid in company income tax on the dividend, which is the 21.43 cents per share or $21.43 in total for our 100 shares. In many cases, this will result in a tax refund from the tax office at the end of the year. In the early years, when each child's investment income is less than $416 (which it will be for the first 10 years or thereabouts under the $1 per day plan), they don't need to lodge a tax return — they just lodge an application for refund of the franking credits and they get a refund cheque from the tax office about two weeks later.

5.3 Choose from many companies

When we buy shares in a company, there is no guarantee that we will get all our money back, or any money back. And there is no guarantee that the company will not reduce dividends or even stop paying dividends altogether. It all sounds rather risky. Not only that, but we have a choice of around 2000 companies listed on the stock exchange that can lose our money for us!

This makes it sound scary, but the reality is not that bad. Companies like ANZ Bank have been around for more than a century and in all likelihood will be around for many decades to come. They will also probably keep growing in value and keep increasing their profits and dividends.

There are many great Australian companies that have been growing successfully for over 100 years and will probably continue to grow for another 100 years. Companies like BHP, Rio Tinto, Westpac, ANZ Bank, AGL and many others. There are also dozens of great companies that are more recent. There are many sources of information about listed companies that can help us assess and select great companies to invest in for our kids' funds. And there are also several ways of investing in a range of companies without having to buy shares in the individual companies themselves.

5.4 Investment returns from shares

The Australian stock market has been generating great returns for investors since it began back in 1875. The stock market consists of around 2000 listed companies, each with its own story and performance. When we hear on the evening news or read in the newspaper that 'the market was down 1.5 per cent today' or 'up 13 per cent last year', that just means that the overall market, averaged across all the listed companies, was up or down by that amount. There are various methods used to measure the overall market, the most well known of which is the All Ordinaries Index, often called the All Ords. The All Ordinaries Index is an index of the prices of the largest 400 or so listed companies on the ASX. The other 1500 or so listed companies are very small and don't influence the overall average.

The All Ordinaries Index is the traditional benchmark used to measure the performance of the stock market as a whole. It measures the capital growth from the sharemarket. (It's like measuring the growth of apple trees, but ignoring the apples and any new trees from replanted apple seeds.) The All Ordinaries Accumulation Index measures total returns from the sharemarket, including capital gains and income. It assumes that all income is reinvested (and therefore 'accumulates'). This is a much better measure of total returns from share investing over time, as it includes the reinvestment of the dividend income, which is what we will be doing in our $1 per day investment funds.

Over long periods, some companies have generated returns of over 20 per cent per year, and some companies have produced very poor returns or even gone backwards. Some companies collapse and go into liquidation (go broke and close up shop) and the shareholders lose some or all of their money. But the overall market has been generating returns of between 10 per cent and 12 per cent for over a century.

As I've mentioned, for our $1 per day plan to grow to $1 million over 50 years, we need to achieve investment returns averaging around 11 per cent per year (which includes capital growth and reinvested income). Most of our funds will be invested in Australian company shares because they provide good growth over the long term.

Figure 5.1 (overleaf) shows the annual total returns (that is, capital growth plus income reinvested) from the Australian sharemarket for each calendar year from 1875 to 2010.

Figure 5.1: returns from Australian shares, 1875–2010

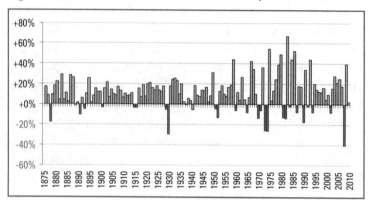

We're in this for the long term, so let's see how the market has performed over the 110 years since Federation:

→ The average return over the whole 20th century was 11 per cent per year, and this included crises such as the Great Depression, both world wars, the 1987 crash and the 2008 global financial crisis.

→ The single best year was 1983, with a return of over 66 per cent.

→ The worst year was 2008, with a 40 per cent loss, and the second worst was 1930, with a loss of nearly 30 per cent.

→ During the 100 years of the 20th century, 22 were negative, so one year in every 4.5 years was a negative year.

→ The longest run of positive returns was 13 years, from 1902 to 1914, when the First World War broke out. After the war, there was a 12-year run of positive returns from 1917 to 1928, when the 'crash of 1929' put an end to that.

→ The longest run of negative returns throughout the whole century was still only two years.

→ Even during the Great Depression in the 1930s, only 1930 and 1938 were negative years. The other years in the Great Depression saw positive returns from shares.

Table 5.2 shows that each decade in the history of the Australian Stock Exchange (and the Sydney Stock Exchange before it) produced overall positive returns.

Table 5.2: past returns from Australian shares (All Ordinaries Accumulation Index)

Decade	Average return (%)	Negative years	Best year		Worst year	
1880s	+14.0	1	1883	+29.0%	1889	-1.1%
1890s	+6.2	2	1895	+25.6%	1891	-10.4%
1900s	+11.7	1	1903	+21.9%	1901	-3.2%
1910s	+7.9	2	1919	+18.7%	1915	-3.5%
1920s	+13.3	1	1922	+21.3%	1929	-5.3%
1930s	+8.5	2	1933	+25.6%	1930	-29.6%
1940s	+8.6	1	1942	+18.4%	1941	-5.5%
1950s	+13.2	2	1959	+44.3%	1952	-13.3%
1960s	+11.6	2	1967	+42.5%	1965	-8.2%
1970s	+6.6	4	1975	+54.6%	1974	-26.2%
1980s	+17.7	4	1983	+66.8%	1982	-13.9%
1990s	+11.1	3	1993	+44.1%	1990	-17.5%
2000s	+8.7	2	2009	+39.6%	2008	-40.4%

Total returns from Australian shares (including re-invested dividends) have averaged 10.8 per cent per year since 1900, 11.3 per cent since the Second World War and 12.4 per cent per year since 1979. These are the types of returns we can expect for our kids' long-term investment funds.

Although past returns are no guarantee of what will happen in the future, some general observations can be made:

→ Over the very long term, returns from the Australian sharemarket have averaged between 10 per cent and 12 per cent per year.

→ There have been a lot more good years than bad years — about one in every three or four years is a negative year. There is no need to panic about a negative year or two, it's normal.

→ There are often long periods, up to a decade or more, of consecutive positive years. The negative runs are very short by comparison. In the 135 years since 1875, when records began in Australia, there have been six negative runs lasting two years, which isn't to say that negative runs longer than two years won't happen in the future. What can be said is that, despite the Depression and two world wars, it's never happened in the history of the stock market in Australia.

→ The 'good' years more than make up for the 'bad' years. In 135 years there have been only four years with returns worse than −25 per cent (−30 per cent in 1930, −25 per cent in 1973, −26 per cent in 1974, and −40 per cent in 2008). Even the so-called crash of 1987 was a loss of only 8 per cent for the 1987 calendar year, and the great crash of 1929 was a loss of only 5 per cent for the 1929 calendar year.

→ In that same 135-year period there have been 21 years with returns of 25 per cent or better. Do we remember them as well as we remember the two or three crashes? Of course not. People are programmed to remember negatives more than positives. We don't remember the years with positive returns of more than 25 per cent simply because there were so many of them.

There have been an incredible 21 years in which returns were better than 25 per cent:

→ 60+ per cent in 1983

→ 50+ per cent in 1975, 1986

→ 40+ per cent in 1959, 1967, 1980, 1985, 1993

→ 30+ per cent in 1950, 1968, 1972, 1979, 1991, 2009

→ 25+ per cent in 1883, 1887, 1888, 1895, 1933, 1963, 2004.

The great crashes that everybody hears about were actually just tiny bumps on the great road to wealth via the sharemarket.

After-tax returns from shares

In table 5.2, the returns shown by the All Ordinaries Accumulation Index assume that all earnings are reinvested and that there is no tax. This is very similar to what our kids' funds will be doing. All our earnings will be reinvested in the fund and we will pay very little tax. As previously mentioned, in the case of income tax the kids should receive tax refunds of franking credits for the first 10 to 15 years or so of the life of their funds, and they pay very low effective tax rates for most of the rest of the time. They will also pay very little capital gains tax because they will rarely sell shares. In many cases, they will find that they will buy shares and hold them forever.

As a result of these tax refunds, the kids' after-tax returns will often be 1 per cent to 1.5 per cent *higher* than the before-tax return from shares. So an 11 per cent before-tax return would translate into a 12 per cent to 12.5 per cent after-tax return.

The All Ordinaries Accumulation Index tracks the performance of the largest listed companies in Australia. The shares in the kids' funds will generate very similar returns because the share investments will mainly be through index exchange-traded share funds and listed investment companies (which I will discuss later in the chapter), which will broadly match the returns from the whole market, with very low costs.

Figure 5.2 shows the All Ordinaries Accumulation Index as it has grown since records first began in 1875.

Figure 5.2: the Australian stock market over 135 years (1875–2005)—All Ordinaries Accumulation Index

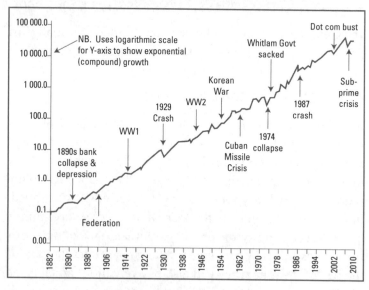

Figure 5.2 shows that there have been four minor hiccups along the long road to wealth via Australian shares:

→ a global depression in the 1890s

→ the Great Depression in the 1930s

→ a major recession in the mid-1970s.

→ the recent sub-prime crisis in 2008–09.

These crises might have appeared serious for the people caught in the middle of them at the time (especially if they borrowed to invest in shares and then lost their jobs and houses as a result, as many did). But figure 5.2 shows that, in the broad scheme of things, they were really just minor hiccups for long-term investors. In each prior crisis the stock market recovered and marched on after only one or two negative years.

I have seen the effects of the two most recent recessions in Australia, in the early 1980s and again in the 1990s — remember Paul Keating's 'recession we had to have'? These resulted in high unemployment, thousands of businesses failing, many thousands of families being thrown out of repossessed houses, streets full of empty shops and boarded-up office buildings. Thousands of people lost their life savings in share schemes, property development schemes and failed mortgage funds, and the recent sub-prime crisis also had its share of collapsed investment schemes and scams.

But take a look at figure 5.2. Can you spot the tiny blips in investment returns from the sharemarket in these recessions? These recessions hardly affected long-term investors. Past returns are no guarantee of what will happen in the future, but with 135 years of history to look at, there is more than a good chance that this pattern will continue in the future. The upward pattern has remained constant throughout this period — through two world wars, depressions, recessions and numerous boom-and-bust cycles, and through a host of dramatic economic, social and technological upheavals. If the market can survive all this, there is a good chance that it will survive just about anything over the next 50 years.

For the purpose of our kids' investment funds we don't need to worry if shares fall in one particular year or in a few years here and there. If our share portfolio is down in one year, we are not going to panic. History shows that the sharemarket will recover and more than make up for losses in future years.

We are looking at a period of 30 to 50 years for our kids' investment funds. Over any given period of 30 to 50 years, Australian shares have produced returns of around 11 per cent or more per year averaged over the period. We can be confident that the sharemarket will do this over the long term because it is driven by several factors that Australian companies have in their favour:

→ steady population growth (more people to buy the products companies produce)

→ productivity growth (increasing profits by doing things smarter and better)

→ good education system, and a good environment for investments in technology and innovation

→ strong global demand for Australian products and services from growing economies, especially in Asia

→ stable legal and tax systems

→ capable management of the economy by the Reserve Bank of Australia and other government departments.

These factors will help ensure that Australian companies (and therefore the sharemarket as a whole) are likely to continue to prosper and provide shareholders with great returns over the long term, just like they have in the past.

5.5 Investing in shares while the fund is still small

As long as the fund is invested in shares of a diverse range of good-quality companies, we can achieve the $1 million target. This is because shares offer greater returns after tax than other major types of investment assets over the long term.

Diversify

As much as we'd like to get into picking shares in individual companies for ourselves and our kids, we probably need around $10 000 or so in the fund before it becomes viable to do that. On the ASX the minimum size transaction for buying shares is $500 per 'parcel', and we need to reduce risk by diversifying across at least a dozen different companies and industry sectors if we are investing in individual companies, so that means we will need several thousand dollars before reaching that stage.

Selecting companies

Another problem with buying shares directly in individual companies in the early years is that it will take time for us to get a feel for the types of companies we want to invest in. It will also take time for us and our kids to learn about the various methods of looking at shares, to develop and understand our own investment style, and to decide which companies to buy. Fortunately there is plenty of time to do this while the fund is still small.

There are, however, a number of ways to invest in shares without actually buying shares in individual companies directly. We can do it by paying other people to select the shares for us, through the following entities.

→ *Managed share funds*. These funds are not listed on the stock exchange and generally require several thousand dollars to start with. They also charge high fees and are not tax-effective.

→ *Unlisted index funds*. These funds have lower fees, but they also require several thousand dollars to start with and are not tax-efficient.

→ *Full-service stockbrokers* (as opposed to online brokers). A full-service broker will require you to have at least $50 000 or so to start with.

→ *Exchange-traded funds*. These funds are ideal for small and large investors, charge very low fees, are tax-efficient, and are listed on the stock exchange so they can be bought in parcels of $500 or more.

→ *Listed investment companies*. These companies are also ideal for small and large investors. Most charge extremely low fees, and they are listed on the stock exchange so they can be bought in parcels of $500 or more.

5.6 Exchange-traded funds

Figure 5.3: basic building blocks

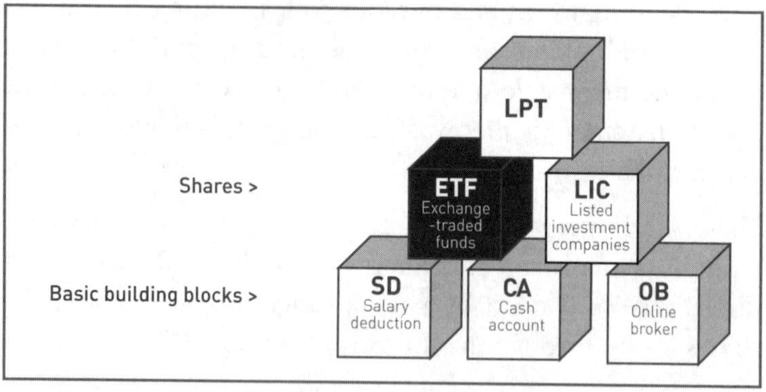

Shares >

Basic building blocks >

LPT

ETF
Exchange-traded funds

LIC
Listed investment companies

SD
Salary deduction

CA
Cash account

OB
Online broker

Exchange-traded funds (ETFs) are an effective way for small investors to have broad exposure to the sharemarket even with small amounts of money and at low cost. They are a relatively recent arrival in Australia but have been operating for decades in North America and Europe.

Index (or 'passive') ETFs aim to match the performance of the index and their fees are low. EFTs are called 'passive' because they don't try to beat the overall market index by constantly buying and selling shares, as the much more expensive 'active' managed funds do. Instead, the passive ETFs just buy all shares in all the companies in the relevant index and only buy and sell shares when the composition of the market index changes. As a result, turnover is low, taxes are low and fees are also very low.

The index ETFs are what we need to focus on for our kids' funds because the fees are very low and their performance tracks very closely with the overall market index returns. Also, we're happy with the returns from the overall sharemarket over the long term.

At the time of writing, there are two broad market ETFs for the Australian stock market, shown in table 5.3.

Table 5.3: broad Australian stock market exchange-traded funds

Provider	Name of fund	ASX code	Index it tracks	Size	Annual fee	Started on ASX
State Street Global Advisors	SPDR 200*	STW	S&P/ ASX 200	$1b	0.29% pa	2001
Vanguard	Vanguard Aust shares ETF*	VAS	S&P/ ASX 300	$5b	0.27% pa	2009

* Distributed semi-annually.

State Street Global Advisors and Vanguard are the largest operators of ETFs in the world, as well as in Australia. State Street has been around for over 200 years in the US and was the first to introduce ETFs in Australia. The SPDR 200 fund is designed to follow the index of the top 200 listed companies.

The Vanguard Australian shares ETF is new to Australia but Vanguard has been the largest operator of unlisted index funds in Australia for many years. The VAS fund tracks the index of the 300 largest listed companies. Both the 200 index and the 300 index are very broad indexes and cover 85 per cent or more of the market value of the entire Australian stock market.

Both of these broad ETFs have matched the overall market very closely, and they have very low fees — just a fraction of the fees of the active managed funds. Before investing, get more information from the product disclosure statement, which can be downloaded from <www. spdrs.com.au> for the SPDR funds and <www.vanguard.com.au> for Vanguard.

Fees on index ETFs are much lower than on active managed funds and even lower than the fees on unlisted index funds. The broad market index ETFs in the above table have no entry fees or exit fees, and have annual management fees of less than 0.30 per cent per year, which is a fraction of the annual fees of active managed funds. ETFs are very similar to unlisted index funds, but they are better for our $1 per day plans because they can be bought using an online broker account, in parcels of as little as $500 — just like any other listed investments — whereas unlisted index funds have minimum investments of around $5000 and are more expensive.

There is little need to diversify across funds and across fund managers because all the index ETFs are doing is 'buying the index'. They are not trying to do anything fancy to beat the index. So, as long as the fund manager is a major, well-known global group (like State Street or Vanguard), we can be reasonably sure that we will go pretty close to matching the performance of the overall market index year after year.

Broad market index ETFs like STW and VAS form the core of our $1 per day plan. We can simply keep putting more money into them as the cash account grows every six months or so. We can keep doing this year after year, decade after decade, without going into any more of the various optional investments we will talk about later. By sticking to the broad market index-based ETFs we could expect to obtain returns virtually the same as those from the general sharemarket, and it would get us to the $1 million target using the $1 per day plan.

Specialised index ETFs

In addition to the two broad market index ETFs just outlined, there are now several more specialised ETFs that are designed to track specific sectors of the Australian market rather than the overall market.

→ State Street offers an ETF that tracks the top 50 index (SFY).

→ State Street offers an ETF that tracks the MSCI high dividend yield index (SYI).

→ Russell also offers an ETF that tracks the high dividend yield index (RDV).

→ Australian Index Investments (Aii) offers a range of ETFs that track sector indexes, including Financials (FIN), Financials excluding property trusts (FIX), Industrials (IDD), Metals and Mining (MAM), Energy (ENY) and Resources (RSR).

These new ETFs enable investors to get quick, low-cost exposure to the companies in these specific subsets of the Australian market without having to buy shares in all the companies in these sectors. These sector ETFs will be very handy later on as the fund grows in size, but in the early years the main priority is to focus on building up the fund with broad market ETFs.

For further information see:

→ State Street Global Advisors SPDR ETFs: <http://www.spdrs.com.au>

→ Vanguard ETFs: <http://www.vanguard.com.au>

→ also visit the ASX site: <www.asx.com.au>.

5.7 Listed investment companies

Figure 5.4: basic building blocks

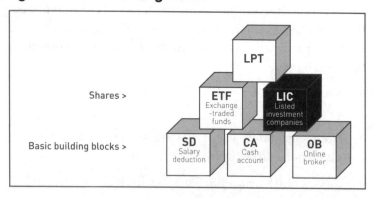

Listed investment companies (LICs) are companies that are listed on the stock exchange, but they use their money to buy shares in other companies listed on the stock exchange. When we buy shares in an LIC, it's almost the same as buying shares in each of the companies that the LIC owns shares in. The advantage is that we can get exposure to lots of companies just by buying shares in one LIC.

LICs are different from index funds or ETFs because LICs aren't passive—they don't try to mirror the All Ordinaries Index exactly but rather try to beat the index. They each have their own investment style, and their performance does not necessarily match the All Ords each year. But, unlike active managed funds, many LICs have demonstrated strong and consistent performance over very long periods of time. Many LICs have track records of 50 years and more, and they have much lower fees than active managed funds.

We still need to diversify

Because LICs don't just replicate the performance of the overall market index, we need to make sure we spread our risk across a couple of different LICs or more. We probably don't need to use a dozen different LICs, but we should pick three or four of the larger ones to spread the risk.

LICs have a number of advantages over active managed funds:

→ *Lower fees*. LICs have no upfront fees, unlike the managed funds. There are no annual management fees, but the LICs do have staff that manage the investments and this costs money. However, the management cost of most LICs is just a fraction of the fees charged by active managed funds and is even lower than those charged by the low-cost index funds. LICs have no exit fees, in contrast to many active managed funds.

→ *No minimum size of investment*. Unlike managed funds, LICs have no minimum investment size. In practice, the minimum parcel size for purchases on the stock exchange is $500.

→ *Generally higher investment performance*. If exactly the same management team ran a managed fund and an LIC, the LIC should do better over the long term because it charges much lower fees. Fees eat into our capital and reduce returns to the investor.

In the funds for our kids we should stick to the large, established LICs, which invest in quality companies for the long term, have low or no borrowings, and have a long record of performance. These are listed in table 5.4.

Table 5.4: major LICs in Australia

Name and website	ASX code	Size	Annual fee (%)	Started
Australian Foundation Investment Co. <www.afi.com.au>	AFI	$4800m	0.16	1936
Argo Investments <www.argoinvestments.com.au>	ARG	$3500m	0.12	1947
Milton Corp. <www.milton.com.au>	MLT	$1600m	0.20	1958
Djerriwarh Investments <www.djerri.com.au>	DJW	$800m	0.36	1995
Australian United Investment Co. <www.aui.com.au>	AUI	$700m	0.18	1953, listed 1974
Choiseul Investments <www.choiseul.com.au>	CHO	$500m	0.15	1990
Diversified United Investment <www.dui.com.au>	DUI	$450m	0.21	1991
Carlton Investments <ph: 02 8234 5000>	CIN	$450m	0.13	1928, listed 1971
Whitefield <www.whitefield.com.au>	WHF	$180m	0.35	1923, listed 1971
Silvastate <www.silvastate.com.au>	SYL	$50m	0.36	1924

This list will change from time to time. However, most of these LICs have been around for several decades and it is likely that they will be around for a long time in the future if they continue with their strategies. Always check their current details on the ASX website, your online broker service or the company websites.

There are also many smaller LICs, most of which specialise in particular types of companies and only arrived on the scene in the last decade. They also tend to charge much higher fees. Since 2004 a great rush of a dozen or more new ones have entered the market. At least for the first several years of our kids' funds, however, we need to stick to the larger, more-established ones listed in table 5.4.

As noted, the LICs listed in table 5.4 have been around for many years and all hold a broad spread of investments. Take a look at the annual fees charged by these LICs. There are several with fees less than 0.20 per cent per year, which is a fraction of the annual fees charged by most active managed funds. And they charge no entry or exit fees either.

I would be happy to use any of these older, larger LICs in the $1 per day plans. We can buy parcels for around $500 or so by buying shares in them through our online broker account. Do some research into the larger LICs and pick one as your first investment. Once we accumulate another $500 or so in the cash account, we can buy into another one — to spread the risk a bit more.

A portfolio consisting of the larger LICs is an easy, low-cost way of investing in the overall sharemarket even for small investors. The portfolio will need very little maintenance — each of the LICs owns a good spread of investments and we can be reasonably sure that the overall returns will be on track with the whole market index over the long term. We don't need to check the share price daily, or even weekly, monthly or quarterly. If our portfolio consisted of three or four, or more, of the larger, more-established LICs, we could sleep easy and be confident that our kids' funds are well on the way to reaching $1 million. All we need to do is keep up with the salary deductions or direct debits, every now and then increase the investments in the LICs from the cash account, and read the half-yearly and annual reports that will be sent in the mail. Keep the dividend statements and use them to do the franking credit refund application or tax return each year, or give them to your tax agent or accountant.

That's it! There's your child's $1 million! A portfolio consisting of index-based ETFs or a selection of the larger, more-established LICs, or both, can be expected to generate the long-term returns needed to reach the $1 million target. There's no need to complicate the investment plan any further if you don't want to. Indeed, I know several investors who have successfully used LICs for many years as their primary method of building wealth over many decades. Many thousands of Australians have used these LICs as their main source of wealth many decades before ETFs arrived on the scene.

5.8 Direct shares

Figure 5.5: basic building blocks

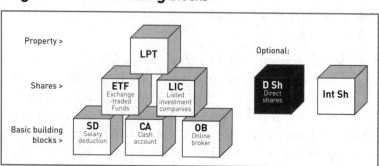

So far I have explored investing in shares through exchange-traded funds and listed investment companies. However, once the kids' funds have grown to at least $10000, we can start to look at investing directly in individual companies. This is purely an optional extra. You would only do this if you and your kids wish to be more involved in the fund.

We don't have to sell our existing ETFs or LICs to invest in direct shares, because we would just have to pay capital gains tax on any increase in value. The ETFs and LICs would still form the backbone of the fund; direct shares would simply add a new dimension to it.

There are a number of advantages to buying shares directly in individual companies, including the following:

→ Lower administration and regulation fees and charges. Once your fund is over $100000 or so you will find that it's even cheaper to run your own broad fund than to pay the (low) ETF and LIC fees.

→ Ability to avoid the 'dud' companies. You can take the time to select your own companies and avoid poor companies with inferior products and management, which drag down the overall market index.

→ Ability to invest in small growth companies. Every large company started out as a struggling small growth stock, and you can spend time researching and investing in small companies that might be destined for great things in the future.

Companies such as BHP, Rio Tinto, Newcrest, Woodside, Santos, Origin Energy, One Steel, Orica, Woolworths, Leightons, Toll, Wesfarmers, AXA, QBE, Coca-Cola Amatil and CSL have each generated returns of more than 11 per cent per year over the past decade (even including the global financial crisis), and many have been around for many decades. There are no guarantees of course that their great performance will continue into the future, but we have plenty of time to do our research and make our own judgments. There are many books on how to assess company shares, including several books written about Australian shares. Some books to get you started are listed at the end of this book. You will have plenty of time to learn about direct shares while the fund is building up the first $10 000 or so in size.

5.9 International shares

Figure 5.6: basic building blocks

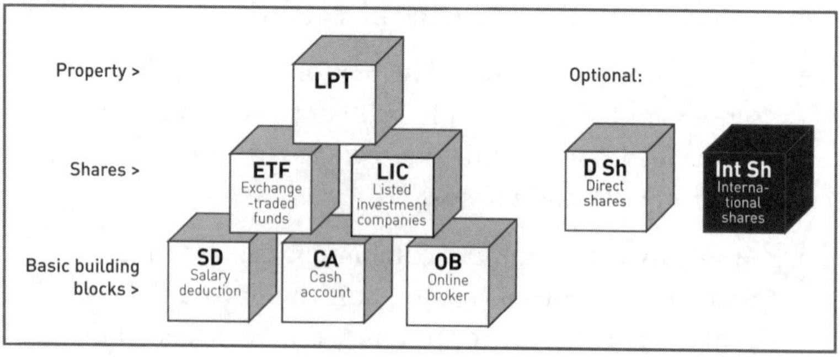

Up to now we have looked at various ways of investing in shares in Australian companies. I began with Australian companies listed on the ASX because they are closest to home and easiest to research. Many of the local companies are household names, such as Woolworths, BHP, Harvey Norman, Fosters and the banks.

Adding some foreign shares to the kids' investment funds is a useful optional extra as the funds grow. International sharemarkets often work in different cycles to the Australian market, so having some of the fund invested in international shares can add to the diversification of the fund and lower the variability of returns to the overall portfolio.

Also, the Australian sharemarket is heavily skewed towards miners and banks, and we need to go to foreign markets to get access to some industry sectors that are under-represented in Australia. Although many Australian companies earn a significant portion of their revenues from overseas, the entire Australian stock market makes up only around 2 per cent to 3 per cent of the global stock market. If we want to invest in companies like Apple, Microsoft, Samsung, LG, Nokia, Ericsson, Nintendo, Johnson & Johnson, Kraft, Heinz, Toyota, Hyundai, Canon, Pepsico, L'Oreal, Estee Lauder, Bayer and thousands of other companies whose products we use every day, we need to go offshore.

A good target would be to have, say, 10 per cent to 30 per cent of the total fund in international shares. Again, international shares are an optional extra; they offer the potential for higher growth and greater diversification, but expect high volatility as well. Since we are in this for the very long term and won't be needing the capital for decades, we are happy to accept the high volatility, and we can also take our time to choose where we want to invest.

How to invest in international shares

Over the past few years the leading global operators of ETFs have listed several of their ETFs covering international stock markets on the ASX. Because they are listed on the ASX, these ETFs can be bought and sold in parcels of as little as $500 just like we buy Australian shares and Australian share ETFs.

The following tables outline the main international share ETFs listed on the ASX, starting with the world excluding the US, as shown in table 5.5 (overleaf).

Table 5.5: world (ex-US) EFTs listed on the ASX

Market	ASX code	Benchmark	Manager	Annual fee	Size	Listed on ASX
World ex-US	VEU*	World ex-US	Vanguard	0.25%	$6b	2009
All countries except the US						
Developed markets ex-US	IVE**	MSCI EAFE	BlackRock iShares	0.35%	$35b	2007
Europe, Far East and Australasia, which is the developed world ex-US. Includes companies like Nestlé, HSBC, Vodafone, BHP, BP, Shell, Toyota, Siemens and Bayer.						

* Distributed annually.
** Distributed semi-annually.

We can narrow the target to particular regions, as shown in table 5.6.

Table 5.6: regional EFTs listed on the ASX

Market	ASX code	Benchmark	Manager	Annual fee	Size	Listed on ASX
Emerging markets	IEM*	MSCI Emerging Markets	BlackRock iShares	0.72%	$45b	2007
BRIC + 23 other emerging markets—good broad mix of growth countries. Includes Samsung, Petrobras, China Mobile, Vale, Taiwan Semiconductor, Infosys and PetroChina.						
Asian tigers	IAA*	S&P Asia 50	BlackRock iShares	0.52%	$200m	2008
4 countries: Hong Kong, South Korea, Taiwan and Singapore. Includes Samsung, Taiwan semi-conductor, Hyundai, HTC and LG.						
UK/Europe	IEU*	Europe 350	BlackRock iShares	0.60%	$1b	2007
Includes Nestlé, HSBC, Vodafone, Shell, Siemens, BASF, Bayer, Daimler, Allianz, Tesco, Barclays, SAP, Danone, Nokia, Ericsson, Carrefour, L'Oreal, Volvo, Michelin, Swatch, Renault, Marks & Spencer and Hermes.						
BRIC— equities	IBK*	MSCI BRIC	BlackRock iShares	0.72%	$1b	2008
Holds the largest stocks in Brazil, Russia, India and China.						

* Distributed semi-annually.

There are also several ETFs that focus on individual countries. These are listed in table 5.7. For most people this would be too specialised, but they do offer very effective ways to get direct access to some great global brands and tap into the growth in the emerging markets.

Table 5.7: country-specific EFTs listed on the ASX

Market	ASX code	Benchmark	Manager	Annual fee	Size	Listed on ASX
China	IZZ*	Xinhua 25	BlackRock iShares	0.73%	$8b	2007
Includes China Mobile, China Life, China Telecom, China Construction Bank, Air China and CNOOC.						
Hong Kong	IHK*	MSCI Hong Kong	BlackRock iShares	0.55%	$2b	2007
Includes Hong Kong Exchanges, Hang Seng Bank, Hutchinson Whampoa, Swire, Henderson Land and Cathay Pacific.						
Japan	IJP*	MSCI Japan	BlackRock iShares	0.56%	$4b	2007
Includes Toyota, Honda, Mitsubishi, Canon, Sony, Panasonic, Nintendo, Nissan, Toshiba, Hitachi, Fujifilm, Fujitsu, Sharp, Ricoh, Kirin and Nikon.						
South Korea	IKO*	MSCI Sth Korea	BlackRock iShares	0.65%	$4b	2007
Includes Samsung, Hyundai, LG, Kia and Daewoo.						
Singapore	ISG*	MSCI Singapore	BlackRock iShares	0.55%	$2b	2007
Includes Singapore Telecom, United Overseas Bank, Genting, Singapore Airlines, Noble, Keppel, Wilmar, and Fraser & Neave.						
Taiwan	ITW*	MSCI Taiwan	BlackRock iShares	0.82%	$3b	2007
Includes Taiwan Semiconductor, HTC, Mediatek, Acer, Advanced Semiconductor, Foxxcon Technology and Powertech.						

* Distributed semi-annually.

The US is still the largest economy in the world, and the US stock market is by far the largest stock market. Table 5.8 shows the five ETFs that track different types of US stocks.

Table 5.8: EFTs specialising in US stocks

Market	ASX code	Benchmark	Manager	Annual fee	Size	Listed on ASX
US—total market	VTS*	US Total market	Vanguard	0.07%	$14b	2009
Probably better over long term than IV—more mid + small caps						
US— big cap	IVV*	S&P500	BlackRock iShares	0.09%	$25b	2007
Ideal to get big cap exposure, since many investors view the S&P500 as the general US equities benchmark						
US— mid cap	IJH*	S&P MidCap 400	BlackRock iShares	0.22%	$8b	2007
The next 400 stocks outside the largest 500 stocks						
US— small cap	IJR*	S&P SmallCap 600	BlackRock iShares	0.20%	$6b	2007
Really mid caps, rather than very small caps						
US— small and micro cap	IRU*	Russell 2000	BlackRock iShares	0.28%	$15b	2007
The smallest 2000 stocks in the Russell 3000 broad index						

* Distributed quarterly.

(The term 'cap' means market capitalisation or market value. So 'big cap' stocks are the largest companies and 'micro-cap' stocks are the smallest companies.) Small cap companies have historically delivered higher returns (but with higher volatility) than big cap stocks.

Investors can also choose to invest in companies specialising in particular global sectors rather than particular countries, as shown in table 5.9.

Table 5.9: EFTs specialising in global sectors

Market	ASX code	Benchmark	Manager	Annual fee	Size	Listed on ASX
Global utities — broad	I00*	Global top 100 stocks	BlackRock iShares	0.40%	$1b	2007
Around 40% are US, and the rest are developed markets. Includes Exxon Mobil, Nestlé, Microsoft, IBM, Procter & Gamble, Johnson & Johnson, General Electric, Intel, Samsung, Walmart and Pepsico.						
Global consumer staples	IXI*	S&P Global Consumer Staples Index	BlackRock iShares	0.48%	$400m	2009
Includes Nestlé, Coca-Cola, Phlip Morris, Walmart, Pepsico, Kraft, Henz, Kellog, Avon, Kirin, Sara Lee, Estee Lauder and Campbell Soup.						
Global healthcare	IXJ*	S&P Global Healthcare Index	BlackRock iShares	0.48%	$500m	2009
Includes Johnson & Johnson, Novartis, Pfizer, Merk, Glaxo, Roche, Bayer and CSL.						
Global telcos	IXP*	S&P Global Teleco Index	BlackRock iShares	0.48%	$300m	2009
Includes AT&T, Vodaphone, Verizon, China Mobile, France Telecom, Deutsche Telekom and Nippon Telegraph & Telephone.						

* Distributed semi-annually.

While the funds are still small, it is usually better to stick to the broader funds that cover several countries. In the funds for my kids we just have just used IEM (iShares Emerging Markets), which is a broad fund that covers the 20 or so countries in the emerging markets, including China, India, Brazil, Russia, and several other emerging markets in Asia, Eastern Europe, Latin America and Africa.

Other broad funds that would benefit from the emerging markets growth include:

→ IAA (iShares Asia 50) — which covers Hong Kong, South Korea, Taiwan and Singapore

→ BRK (iShares BRIC) — which covers Brazil, Russia, India and China.

Investors who wanted to cover the whole world stock market would do it with a combination of VTS (US total market) and VEU (all world excluding US) in a ratio of about one-third to two-thirds; that is, if you were investing $10 000, you would use $3000 of VTS and $7000 of VEU, because the US comprises about a third of the world market.

Currency

When investing in foreign companies (including through an ETF), there are two types of returns: we gain if the share price (and dividends) rise over time, and we also gain if the foreign currency rises against the Australian dollar. On the other hand, if the foreign share price rises but the foreign currency falls, the gains in the share price might be wiped out by losses on the currency.

For this reason we generally buy foreign ETFs when the Australian dollar is high — say, more than 80 to 90 US cents. When the Australian dollar is low (say, less than 70 to 80 US cents), it is often better to buy local shares. Our kids' funds are not in the business of buying or selling our ETFs frequently to try to take advantage of currency changes. We are long-term holders, so it's good to buy foreign shares when the Australian dollar is high and our dollar goes further.

For more information on global shares ETFs listed on the ASX have a look at:

→ Vanguard: <http://www.vanguard.com.au>

→ BlackRock iShares: <http://au.ishares.com/index.do>.

New ETFs are being listed all the time, so it pays to check the ASX site for details: <www.asx.com.au>

5.10 Buying investments on the ASX

The first investment as part of the $1 per day plan is most likely going to be an exchange-traded fund or a listed investment company. Both of these are bought through the ASX using the online broker account. ETFs have units, whereas LICs have shares, but both types of securities can be bought in exactly the same way. I will use the term 'shares' rather than securities, because shares is more common.

Once you have done your homework and decided that you want to buy XYZ shares/units, and you have estimated the share price you will want to buy them at, the next step is to actually buy them. There's no need to rush into it. Remember, we are doing this for the very long term. Take your time so you don't make any mistakes.

How many shares?

The first thing to do is work out how many shares (or units, in the case of ETFs) you want to buy. If your purchase is going to be around $1000 and the share price today is around $20, you are going to be buying 50 shares ($1000 ÷ 20). You also need to allow for brokerage of around $20 (or whatever your online broker charges), which usually includes GST. Make it a nice round number of shares if you can. Also, don't spend all your cash. Leave enough in the cash account just in case the price you get is a bit higher than the price on the screen.

Current price

On the trading screen, type in the code of the stock you want to buy. The screen will show the last sale price, the opening price (first trade of the day), the closing price (the last sale yesterday), the volume of shares traded today and other information about the day's trades.

There should be an indicator for 'Recent announcements' or 'News'. Always check this information to make sure that your company hasn't just announced a huge loss or wasn't taken over the previous night!

'At market' or 'limit' orders

Type in the number of shares you want to buy. On the order screen you will be asked whether the order is to be 'at market' or 'limit'. An at market order means that your shares will be bought at whatever the market price is the moment the order hits the market. A limit order is an order to buy or sell shares where you set a limit for the maximum price you want to pay for the shares (or the minimum price you want to sell the shares for).

Let's say you want to buy 50 XYZ shares. You look at the 'market depth' section of the order screen. Market depth is the list of buyers and sellers in the market at various buying and selling prices. You will find them on all online trading services. An example of market depth is shown in table 5.10.

Take a look at the first row on the buyers' side. There are two buyers in the market who want to buy a total of 100 shares in XYZ for a maximum price of $20.00 per share. In the next row, there is one buyer who wants to buy 1500 shares for $19.90 per share, then six people who want to buy a total of 1000 shares for $19.80 per share and so on.

Table 5.10: market depth

Buyers			Sellers		
2	100	$20.00	2	500	$20.10
1	1 500	$19.90	1	1 200	$20.20
6	1 000	$19.80	15	9 850	$20.30
4	500	$19.70	7	2 250	$20.40
22	14 350	$19.60	31	22 052	$20.50

On the sellers' side, there are two people wanting to sell a total of 500 shares for $20.10, followed by one seller who wants to sell 1200 shares for $20.20 and so on. If you made your buy order for 50 shares an 'at market' order, it would be matched up with the sellers at the lowest price — at $20.10. The instant this happened your buy order would be executed and the sellers at $20.10 would drop to 450 shares, because 50 had been sold to you. This takes just a few seconds.

On the other hand, you might like to make your purchase a limit order and set a limit of, say, $19.90. This means the order goes into the system and is added to the list of sellers. The second row on the buyers' side of the market depth will become two buyers for a total of 1550 shares, as shown in table 5.11.

Table 5.11: a limit order in the market depth

Buyers			Sellers		
2	100	$20.00	2	500	$20.10
2	**1 550**	**$19.90**	1	1 200	$20.20
6	1 000	$19.80	15	9 850	$20.30
4	500	$19.70	7	2 250	$20.40
22	14 350	$19.60	31	22 052	$20.50

This means that the shares will only be bought after the 100 shares at $20.00 are bought, and after the first 1500 shares for $19.90 are bought. Then your 50 shares at $19.90 will be bought. This, of course, assumes that there are lots of sellers wanting to sell their shares for these prices. If the pricing is moving down during the day, this might take a minute or two. Or if the price is moving up at the time, it may not get down to $19.90. In reality, for large companies the share price generally moves both up and down by half a per cent or so during the day. So the chances of your shares being bought at $19.90 are pretty good.

By using a limit order instead of an at market order, you will have bought your shares at $19.90 instead of $20.10, which is 20 cents per share less and amounts to 1 per cent less of the purchase price. This might not sound like much, but it's these sorts of little differences that add up to a fortune over time.

Therefore, take plenty of time to research and select the ETF or the companies you want to own and think about how much you are prepared to pay for them. If you are buying shares in a company that turns over hundreds of thousands or even millions of shares every day (check the volume figure next to the share price), and if the market depth shows lots of buyers and sellers around the selling price, this is what's called a 'liquid' market — there are plenty of buyers and sellers. Make the order at market so it's done as quickly as possible.

If the company you are buying into doesn't have large numbers of buyers and sellers around the share price, it might take some time to fill your order. In this case you can make your order a limit order and put a maximum price limit on it. If you have chosen a reasonable limit price (fairly close to the last sale price), it might take a couple hours to fill the order.

If your shares remain unbought at the end of the day, they will stay on the market for your set limit price for as long as you want them to. On the order screen you will be asked how long the limit order is to remain current. Some brokers have a maximum of 30 days.

Best time of day

Most shares are traded in the first half-hour of the trading day (10.00 am to 10.30 am) and in the last half-hour (3.30 pm to 4.00 pm), which means that the market depth is often best around these times, so the spreads will usually be smaller. The 'spread' is the difference between the lowest seller's price and the highest buyer's price. The market opens between 10.00 am and 10.10 am, with companies coming on in alphabetical order. So, if you want to buy shares in Zinifex, for example, it won't open until around 10.09 am. For your first few transactions it's best not to start too close to 4.00 pm because you might not get through the process before the market closes. Start at about 3.00 pm and take plenty of time. You don't want to be rushed into making mistakes.

Executing the order

Once you have placed your buy order, the stock exchange computer matches it with a sell order for the same number of shares and executes the order. Sometimes this takes a fraction of a second, but sometimes it can take hours. It all depends on how many other buyers and sellers there are in the market and what prices they want for their orders. Generally, we will be sticking to large companies with large volumes of shares traded each day, so the orders will take seconds or minutes, not hours. That's it! You're a shareholder — almost.

5.11 What happens after you buy shares?

A number of things take place after a purchase of shares:

→ Your trade will appear on the executed orders list.

→ A contract note will be emailed to you.

→ Your portfolio will be updated.

→ Settlement will occur.

→ Share registry forms will be sent to you.

→ A CHESS holding statement will be mailed to you.

Executed orders

Usually, by the time you get out of the order screen and find your way to the executed orders screen, the deal should already have been done and your completed trade should appear in the executed orders list. Check that you bought the right number of shares and at the price you wanted. Make sure that you actually bought shares and didn't *sell* shares by mistake (as I did once!). It's very nasty when you sell shares you don't even own. If that happens, you need to quickly buy them back the same day, hopefully at a profit — hey, you're a day trader already!

Contract note

Most online brokers send a contract note to the nominated email address. Print the contract note out and check the number of shares, the price and the brokerage. Also, check the bottom, where it will say something like 'cash to be taken from nominated account'. This means that their computer knows that the cash will automatically come from the linked cash account. If the contract note says something like 'needs cleared funds to settle', it sounds like it's expecting you to bring in a bank cheque. Ring the broker to make sure the automatic cash account link is set up properly. If you are in any doubt, it pays to ring the broker and double-check.

Portfolio update

A few minutes after the contract note has been sent your new shareholding will appear in the portfolio under 'Current shareholdings'. If the portfolio screen also shows the current cash balance in the linked cash account, it will show that the $1000 purchase price plus $20 in brokerage is still in the account. This is not a mistake. The $1020 will stay in the cash account until settlement.

Settlement

When securities are bought through the ASX, we actually pay for them three business days after the order is executed — this is called 'T+3 settlement'. (Likewise, when securities are sold, the money arrives in the cash account three business days later.) Three days after you have bought the shares, you will need to have cleared funds in the cash account in order to pay for the shares. When you opened the trading account you will have specified that all trades are to be settled from the cash account — that is, money to buy shares automatically comes out of the cash account and money received from the sale of shares is automatically credited to the account.

When the cash account statement arrives at the end of the month, there will be a debit for the $1020, or whatever the purchase price was, plus brokerage. Check the details to make sure they are correct.

Share registry forms

About a week after buying shares in a company, the share registry will send several forms in the mail:

→ *Tax file number form*. You will need to provide either your TFN or your child's TFN. You must supply a valid TFN; otherwise, the share registry will deduct income tax and 'withhold it', and send it to the Tax Office.

→ *Annual report request*. Most companies send an annual report request to allow us to choose whether or not to receive an annual report at the end of the year, and other reports, such as half-yearly or quarterly reports, during the year. The annual report and other reports are very useful and you should read them. You will learn more and more about the companies you're investing in by reading these reports.

→ *Direct credit for dividends*. The direct credit for dividends form requests the details of the cash account so any dividends or other distributions go straight into it.

→ *Dividend reinvestment form*. Many large companies have a dividend reinvestment plan (DRP). This enables shareholders to reinvest the dividends or distributions (in the case of an ETF) back into the company (or fund). For long-term investment plans where the income is not going to be spent, DRPs are a good idea. Some-times there is a discount on the entry price (up to 5 per cent or more) and we get to invest without paying any brokerage.

CHESS holding statement

At the end of the month a Clearing House Electronic Subregister System (CHESS) holding statement will arrive in the mail, telling you that you bought 50 shares in XYZ. This is the computer that automatically processes the paperwork for the transactions on the ASX. When we buy shares we don't get a share certificate any more, we get a CHESS holding statement showing what shares we own. We receive one statement for each company or investment. Check all the details and make sure they are correct, and file the CHESS statement for future reference.

If and when you sell some or all of the shares in XYZ, you will also receive a CHESS statement showing the number of shares you sold and the balance remaining. File all statements you receive on each company together so the entire history of your holdings in each company is together. That's it—your first investment is in the bag. You're on your way!

5.12 How often should you check the share price?

Now that you've bought your shares, it's extremely tempting to look at the share price straightaway, just to see how it is going. Don't look at the share price and try to stop the kids from doing it as well. It's irrelevant. If you bought one of the major ETFs or LICs, the price is 'even more' irrelevant. The investment will jump up and down along with the overall sharemarket, day after day, month after month, year after year, decade after decade. That's why you bought them—so you wouldn't need to worry about the share price all the time.

If you're at the stage of buying individual company shares, you shouldn't worry about the share price day to day or month to month either. As a part owner in a company, what you should be worrying about is how the company's business is going, not its share price. You should only want to sell the shares if something major affected the company's ability to keep growing earnings like it has in the past. You should have only bought the shares after spending time researching the company, so don't be worried about minor ups and downs in the share price. The half-yearly and annual reports, which include the auditor's report, the accounts and the director's report, are what you should be interested in. If you're happy with those things, the share price will take care of itself in the long term.

So forget the share price and concentrate on the next investment!

Should we set a price 'target'?

Many investors say that a price target should be set when buying shares. They set a target price for the shares and, if the share price reaches the target, they sell the shares. The idea is that they try to take a profit when the price has reached the target, just in case the price later falls and they lose the opportunity to take the profit.

For example, my son was born in August 2000. At that time BHP shares were $8.50. We could have said to ourselves, 'We would be really happy if the shares grow 20 per cent over the next year so we will set a price target of $10.20, and we should aim to sell if the price reaches $10.20.' Sure enough, the share price did move up to $10.20, by May 2001. If we had sold the shares then, we would have made a tidy profit of 20 per cent — not bad for nine months.

But we didn't sell because we hadn't set a price target. We bought BHP because we believed that it was going to generate long-term returns of at least 10 per cent to 12 per cent per year over the long term — and we mean very long term. Unless something goes radically wrong with BHP's business, we expect to hold the shares forever. BHP has been listed on the

ASX for over a century, and we expect that these shares will still be part of our son's fund when he reaches his $1 million target in 40 or 50 years' time.

When BHP reached $10.20 in May 2001, nothing had changed within the BHP business that radically affected its ability to generate the kinds of returns we were looking for, so we didn't sell the shares. If we had sold BHP, we would have had to pay tax on the capital gain, and we would have had to find another good company to invest the remaining money in.

The company kept marching on to bigger and better things. The share price hit $50 in May 2008 but then plummeted to $20 by November 2008 in the depths of the 'global financial crisis'. We didn't panic and sell this time either. China, India and most other emerging markets were still growing strongly and BHP's business was still strong, despite the share price. As the world recovered from the GFC, the share price recovered to more than $40 and the business still looks fine. Over the whole decade the returns from BHP have been over 20 per cent per year — which is well above our long-term target of 11 per cent. If we had panicked and sold in either 2001 or 2008, we would have missed out on most of that tremendous growth.

For this reason we don't set price targets — we buy shares as if we are never going to sell them. We ignore the share price and focus on whether or not the *business* keeps growing, regardless of what the share price might do from time to time.

Should we set a 'stop loss'?

Many advisers say that it's important to set a stop loss whenever we buy shares. For example, when we bought the BHP shares for $8.50, we could have set a 'stop loss' price of $8. This means that if the share price drops below $8, we should sell at that point, in order to stop our losses from getting any worse. The share price might continue to fall, so we are better off getting out at $8 rather than suffering more losses. These days it's possible to set up an automatic stop loss order on many broker accounts, so when the price drops below the stop loss order price, the computer will automatically sell the shares. Some broker services offer price alerts sent to the customer's mobile phone when prices reach a set level. This all sounds very convenient, but in fact it can be very dangerous.

For long-term investors, the problem with stop loss orders is that they can sell us out at the worst possible time and prevent us from making any profits in the future. For example, shortly after BHP reached $10.20 in mid-2001, the whole market fell over the next six months and BHP had dropped to well below $8 by September 2001 (as a result of the September 11 terrorist attacks in the US). Just because the price dropped below some arbitrary level, should we have sold out at, say, $8.00 in order to stop our losses from getting worse? Of course not — nothing had changed our view of the BHP business. It was a fine company producing a wide range of resources and selling them to customers all over the world, just like it had been a few months earlier when the price was over $10. In fact, the share price dropped even further, to around $7.50, but then it started its long rise to above $40. If we had panicked and sold for $7.50 in September 2001, we would have made a loss of 12 per cent on the investment. But we kept the shares and now they have gained more than 400 per cent in value.

We only need to sell shares when something in the business changes, not when the share price drops. Too many irrelevant factors affect share prices, so don't look at the price all the time to try to work out what's going on.

If your investments are ETFs or some of the larger LICs, it makes even less sense to set up price targets and stop losses.

You can expect the price to drift up and down from week to week, month to month or year to year. Leave the investments alone and worry about other things. They will be fine — they will be the ones that get you to $1 million. We will talk about what to do when markets go through booms and busts in chapter 7.

Chapter 6

Property investments

6.1 Property

Figure 6.1: basic building blocks

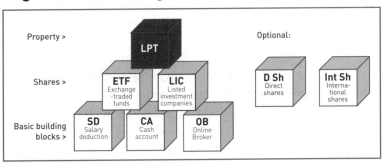

Along with shares, the other main class of investment asset that can generate good long-term growth is property. If you look at any list of wealthy people in Australia (for example, the annual *BRW* Rich 200 list) you will find that about a quarter to a third of them made their money from property. It hasn't been from residential property (housing), however; it has been from the ownership and/or development of commercial property.

There are several categories of commercial property, including:

→ offices

→ shops — including retail shopping centres

→ industrial — warehouses

→ tourist accommodation — hotels and resorts

→ aged care — retirement and nursing homes.

Commercial property trusts make up around 10 per cent of the overall share market index in Australia, so just by buying a broad share investment (like a broad Australian share ETF) you will be getting some exposure to the commercial property sector. You may, however, wish to have an additional allocation to property — because of the benefits property provides in certain conditions. You don't have to include a separate allocation to property in your investment funds, but it is worth remembering that many thousands of Australians (including me) have made a lot of money over several decades by investing in firms such as Westfield and Stockland — which are still around today. Having property in the fund is not essential (like shares are), but well-located, well-managed property, bought at the right time, can be a useful addition to long-term portfolios.

There is no right or wrong way to put your child's fund together. Whether it consists mainly of shares plus a bit of property, or has no separate property allocation, if you do some homework and take care when selecting the investments, you are likely to reach the $1 million target. One thing is certain — if the fund is invested mainly in bank accounts, term deposits, debentures or mortgage funds, you will not reach $1 million.

As with investing in companies, small investors don't need to buy whole properties in order to invest in property. There are many property trusts and funds that provide small investors with exposure to a huge variety of property types. For as little as $500 you can buy a small stake in a trust that owns hundreds of different properties.

6.2 Property versus shares

Throughout history, most of the world's wealth has been created through ownership of companies, and that is why shares generally make up the bulk of long-term investment portfolios.

Nonetheless, property does offer some advantages over shares; the main advantages are listed here.

→ *Hedge against inflation.* While shares offer some protection against moderate inflation, property generally provides better protection in periods of high inflation. For example, in the high-inflation environment of the 1970s in Australia and many other countries, shares did very poorly while well-located properties did a much better job of holding their value in real terms after inflation. This is because rents (and therefore property values) for well-located properties generally rise with inflation.

→ *Less bankruptcy risk.* Every day of the week a company somewhere goes bankrupt because it runs out of money. Companies are essentially built on ideas, with very little in the way of hard assets of any lasting value. If management can't capitalise on these ideas by getting customers to pay more for the product or service than it costs to produce it, the company will close and the owners (shareholders) will lose their investment. In the case of property, the assets are the land and buildings, which can almost always be sold. This doesn't mean, of course, that property trusts can't fail if they borrow too much — a couple did fail during the global financial crisis — but this is a much rarer event than companies failing.

→ *Supply and demand.* Well-located properties in areas of growing population and growing incomes will generally do well. Australia is almost unique in the world in having a growing population that has been concentrated in a small number of cities that have grown consistently in population and income levels for the past two centuries. This trend of high population growth (mainly through immigration) and high concentration is likely to continue for the foreseeable future. Properties located in or near the centre of these growing cities are hard to duplicate, and this keeps their values growing. It is hard to build a dozen more Chatswoods and Bondi Junctions in Sydney, Chadstones and Collins Streets in Melbourne, Queen Streets in Brisbane, and so on.

6.3 Listed property funds and trusts

Listed property trusts (LPTs) are also called REITs (real estate investment trusts, or A-REITs in the case of Australian REITs).

Their units are listed on the stock exchange and can also be bought and sold through online broker accounts. Their unit prices are included in the share price listings in the finance section of most newspapers. LPTs are a bit like listed investment companies (LICs), except that they invest in properties instead of shares in other companies.

6.4 The main listed property trusts

Table 6.1 sets out the larger listed property funds in Australia. They change from time to time, so check *The Australian Financial Review*, your online broker account or the ASX website <www. asx.com.au> for current information.

Table 6.1: the main listed property funds in Australia

Name of fund	ASX code	Approx size	Listed	Types of properties	Countries
Westfield Group <www.westfield. com>	WDC	$18 billion	1961	retail	Australia, US, UK
Westfield Retail <www.westfield. com>	WRT	$12 billion	2010	retail	Australia, NZ
Stockland <www.westfield. com>	SGP	$9 billion	1987	diversified	Australia
GPT <www.gpt.com.au>	GPT	$5 billion	1971	diversified	Mostly Aust, some US
Colonial First State Retail <www.colonialfirst state.com.au/cfx>	CFX	$5 billion	1994	retail	Australia
Mirvac <www.mirvac.com. au>	MGR	$4 billion	1999	diversified	Australia

Table 6.1 *(cont'd)*: the main listed property funds in Australia

Name of fund	ASX code	Approx size	Listed	Types of properties	Countries
Goodman Group <www.goodman.com>	GMG	$4 billion	2005	industrial	Half in Aust, rest in US, Europe, Asia
Dexus Property Group <www.dexus.com.au>	DXS	$4 billion	2004	office, industrial	Mostly Aust, some US, Europe
Colonial First State Office <www.colonialfirststate.com.au/cpof>	CPA	$2 billion	1999	office	Australia
ING Office fund <www.ingrealestate.com.au>	IOF	$2 billion	2000	office	Half Aust, rest in US, Europe
Australand <www.australand.com.au>	ALZ	$2 billion	1997	diversified	Australia
Charter Hall Office <www.charterhall.com.au/cqo>	CQO	$1 billion	1993	office	US, Australia
ING Industrial fund <www.ingrealestate.com.au>	IIF	$1 billion	1991	industrial	Australia, Europe
Charter Hall Retail <www.charterhall.com.au/cqr>	CQR	$1 billion	1995	retail	Mainly Aust, some in US
Bunnings Warehouse Property Trust <www.bwptrust.com.au>	BWP	$1 billion	2004	retail	Australia
Abacus Property Group <www.abacusproperty.com.au>	ABP	$1 billion	2002	diversified	Australia

These funds are all big funds with many thousands of investors. Use the ASX codes to look a few of them up on your online broker website or the ASX website and learn more about them. The fund websites contain information about the funds, including annual reports, prospectuses and product disclosure statements, which can be downloaded or ordered online.

Many of these firms have been around for many decades and have survived recessions and property downturns, including the recent global financial crisis, in which some of the more highly geared property trusts failed. I discuss some of the things to look out for below.

A good way to get started in the listed property sector is to invest in an exchange-traded fund that buys into a range of LPTs. Currently there are two in Australia; these are shown in table 6.2.

Table 6.2: ETFs that buy into LPTs*

Name of fund	ASX code	Bench-mark	Manager	Annual fee	Size	Listed on ASX
SPDR S&P/ ASX 200 Listed Property Fund <www.spdrs. com.au>	SFL	ASX/S&P A-REIT Index	State Street Global Advisors	0.40%	$0.3b	2002
Vanguard Australian Property Securities Index ETF <http://au. ishares.com>	VAP	ASX/S&P A-REIT Index	Vanguard	0.34%	$2b	2010

* Distributed quarterly.

These ETFs are designed to track the Property Trust Index, which is the index that reflects the performance of the largest dozen or so property trusts listed on the ASX (in the same way that other ETFs are designed to track the All Ordinaries Index). This would be a simple and inexpensive way to get exposure to the whole listed property market. Download a product disclosure statement from either or both websites to learn how these ETFs operate and to inform yourself of the current holdings, fees and so on.

When to buy

Once a few thousand dollars of your child's fund has been invested in shares, you may wish to start to invest in listed property. Do some homework into the larger, more diversified funds and select what seem to you to be the best two or three. Or you can start with one of the property ETFs, which would save you having to diversify across several funds. Use your online broker account to buy units in property ETFs or property funds in the same way as you would buy shares.

Just as there are optimal times to buy global shares (when the Australian dollar is high), there are also optimal times to buy listed property. If you have decided to buy listed property funds, then it is best to do it when unit prices are at a discount in relation to the value of the properties owned by the funds.

For example, if a listed fund owns property worth $1 billion (net of debt) and has one billion units on issue, then the units should trade at around $1 per unit. However, from time to time the units might actually trade at a 10 per cent or even 20 per cent discount to the 'book value' of the underlying properties. The share listings in the major newspapers list the 'book value' (B/V) or 'price/book ratio' (P/B or P/BV ratio) for all companies and trusts listed on the stock exchange. This is also knows as the Net Asset Value (NAV), which is also shown on the funds' websites.

If the net book value or NAV is $1 per unit but the units are trading at 90 cents, the price-to-book ratio (or price-to-NAV ratio) will be shown as 0.9, meaning that you can buy it at a discount of 10 per cent below the net market value of the properties.

Another similar measure published in the newspapers and on websites is the price to 'net tangible assets' (NTA). Net tangible assets are all hard assets (like property) less all debts, and for property trusts the NTA is similar to the net book value. If the price to NTA is less than 1.0, then the units are trading at a discount to the net value of the properties.

The book value is based on the market value of each property as valued by registered property valuers, but don't rely solely on this. Each firm's annual report and website usually include a detailed report on each property and its valuation. If you have decided to buy listed property and you are happy with the valuations at $1 per unit, then why not buy when you can get it for 90 cents per unit or even less (that is, when the price-to-book value is less than 1)?

On the other hand, there are also times when property trusts trade at a premium to their book value, meaning that the units are trading at more than the value of their underlying properties. This is often the case in booms, when rents are inflated or investors are overly optimistic about the prospects for the economy or the properties in the trust. This is usually a sign that the units are overpriced and means it's a good time to hold off on buying. If the trust managers can't convince the property valuers that the properties are worth more, then I don't usually want to pay more either.

Apart from the book value issue, a second critical issue is the level of debt. One of the great advantages (and potential dangers) of investing in property is that banks generally love lending against property. Property owners (including listed property trusts) often fall into the trap of borrowing too much during booms, and this almost always ends in tears when the boom ends.

Investors in property trusts should always be wary of debt levels that exceed around 30 per cent to 40 per cent of the properties' value. In the boom leading up to the 2008 global financial crisis, the debt levels of several of the major trusts reached or even exceeded 60 per cent, and these trusts suffered badly in the credit crisis. Always stick to trusts with debt levels no higher than around 40 per cent of the properties' value. Details of debt levels can be found in the research section of online brokers and in the annual reports and other information available on property trust websites.

6.5 Investment returns from property

Looking back over the history of investment returns in Australia, the average returns from property (listed property trusts) and companies (listed shares) have been similar. Over the past 30 years, shares have returned around 12 per cent per year and property trusts have returned around 10 per cent per year. These are average returns over the long term, but of course there are good years and bad years along the way.

The average returns figures are for the industry as a whole. We can do better than these returns for both property and shares if we do some homework and learn how to choose the better companies and the better property funds — and avoid the duds. But in the early years of our kids' funds we need to stick to broad property trusts and share funds that more or less follow the indexes.

The returns from property investments listed on the Australian Stock Exchange have been measured by the Property Trust Accumulation Index since the end of 1979. Just like the All Ordinaries Accumulation Index, the Property Trust Accumulation Index measures total returns, which include both capital growth and income, assuming that all income (that is, dividends from shares and distributions from property trusts) is reinvested.

From the start of the indexes in 1979 to the year 2010, total returns from property trusts averaged 10 per cent per year (compared with 12 per cent per year from Australian shares), despite the big losses during the recent global financial crisis. This is shown in figure 6.2.

Figure 6.2: shares versus listed property, 1979 to 2010

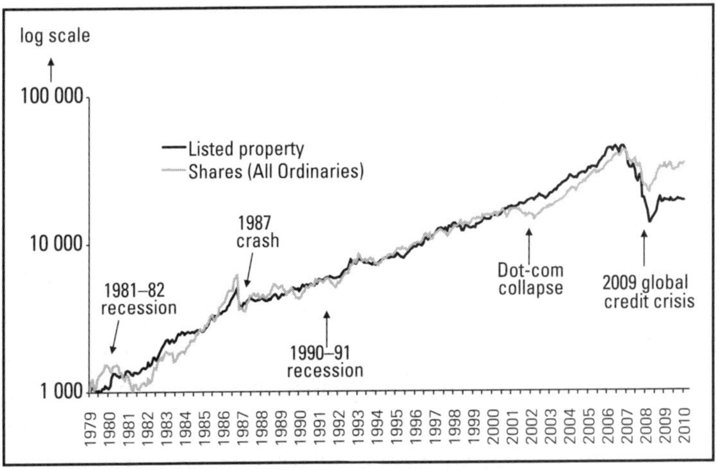

Although returns from listed property have been a little lower than those from shares, the overall ride for portfolios that include property as well as shares has been a little smoother than for those with shares alone. Some of the reasons for this are listed here.

→ Over the 31-year period from 1979 to 2010, the Listed Property Index suffered losses in only four years, compared with nine years of losses from shares.

→ Property had seven years where returns were lower than 5 per cent, compared with 11 years for shares.

→ Although shares suffered losses in nine of the 31 years, property had positive returns in seven of these nine years, and there were only two years in which both shares and property were down — 1994 and 2008.

However, in 2008, which was the worst single year for both property and shares, returns from property fell to −54 per cent, while that from shares didn't drop quite as much, falling to −40 per cent. The year 2008 was certainly a bad year all around, but long-term investors who focus on quality trusts — with low debt levels — and try to buy into them when units are trading at a discount will ride out the ups and downs in the market and achieve their target over the long term.

6.6 Tax benefits of property

Overall, property tends to produce higher income and lower capital growth than shares. Averaged over very long periods, the Australian sharemarket has tended to produce income (dividends) of around 4 per cent per year, plus capital growth of around 7 per cent. Property funds, on the other hand, have produced income (called distributions) of around 7 per cent to 8 per cent per year on average, plus capital growth of around the inflation rate or a little lower, so the mix between income and capital gains is very different.

The higher levels of income earned by property investments is not necessarily good for long-term investers like us, because we will need to pay tax each year on income. In the case of companies, most listed companies pay dividends that are fully or partly franked and the return from dividends is only 3 per cent or 4 per cent per year, so the income tax is very low. We have already seen that we can get tax refunds for the tax already paid by the company, so the kids will often get tax refunds instead of paying tax.

In the case of property trusts and funds, most of them also have tax benefits attached to their distributions to unit holders. If we own units in a property trust or fund, we will receive an annual statement at the end of each year outlining the distributions for the year and any tax benefits attached to them. Generally, a portion of the distributions will be tax-deferred, meaning that we won't need to pay tax on this part of the distribution until we sell the units, which may occur in many years' time or in retirement, when we are in a low tax bracket.

The portion of tax-deferred income in each trust changes each year, so it can't be predicted accurately. The effect of receiving tax-deferred income is that part of our tax bill can be not only reduced but also postponed for many years, perhaps forever. This reduces our overall tax rate significantly in the meantime and allows us to keep more money in the fund to reinvest.

The bottom line is this—for investors who pay tax, the after-tax returns from most property funds are probably going to be around 1 per cent or 2 per cent lower than the before-tax returns. In the case of our kids, they will not be paying any tax on their investment income for around the first 20 years under the $1 per day plan. The property ETFs and many of the property funds do distribute a small amount of their distributions as franked dividends, and these can generally be refunded to the investor. Therefore, the after-tax returns will be the same or even a little higher than the before-tax returns from property funds. Therefore, their after-tax returns will be the same as their before-tax returns from property funds.

6.7 Unlisted property funds and trusts

In addition to the listed property trusts we discussed earlier, there are unlisted property funds (trusts). We can't buy or sell unlisted investments through the stock exchange and we can't look up the unit price every day (or every minute). They are similar to managed funds in that we buy units by filling out an application form and sending a cheque to the property fund manager. We can sell units by applying to the property fund manager for a withdrawal. The unit prices of unlisted property trusts are valued regularly and published in newspapers and on the property fund managers' websites.

I recommend we use only listed property trusts as the main type of property investment in the $1 per day plan because of the many advantages they have over unlisted property funds. These include liquidity (being able to buy and sell any day), low fees, low entry cost and transparency on the stock exchange. Also, most unlisted funds have minimum entry amounts of several thousand dollars.

Chapter 7

How the fund grows over time

In this chapter I outline what the kids' investment funds should look like over the years. The size of the fund at each stage is based on contributions of $1 per day and assumes that no initial lump sum was deposited to open the account. In practice, the fund balances will probably be larger than this if you:

→ open the account with a lump sum

→ increase the regular contributions at a faster rate

→ make additional contributions from time to time, such as money from Christmas or birthdays. If any contributions such as these are made, on top of the $1 per day, the fund will grow at a much faster rate and end up with a much bigger total.

7.1 Year 1—under $500

The three basic building blocks of the plan are set up in the first year:

→   cash account (see sections 3.7–3.12)

→   salary deductions or direct debits (see section 2.8)

→   online broker account (see sections 3.13–3.15).

You can also apply for the kids' tax file numbers. This will involve a lot of searching around for information and filling out of forms. Unfortunately there is no way around this, but once it's done you won't have to do it again. These three components form the basis of the plan for the next several decades.

That's it for the first year. Get these basic steps done and concentrate on raising the kids until the fund gets above $500 or so. Whenever possible you should try to add to the account, whether money from Christmas or birthday presents, part of your annual bonus, if you get one, or part of the baby bonus. Every little bit helps.

7.2 Years 2 to 5—$500 to $3000

Once the fund is above $500, you can start putting the money to work. Cash is not a growth asset and the interest income will become taxable each year before long. So you need to get the money working harder—by investing it in growth investments with some tax advantages. There will always be some money in the cash account. This account will keep collecting the contributions from the salary deductions or direct debits from your bank account, plus dividends and distributions from the investments. It is also useful to have some cash in any investment plan because it may be needed to buy other investments when the opportunity arises. If you have some cash in the account, you won't need to sell an investment (and maybe pay capital gains tax on it) in order to buy into a new investment.

When the fund is above $500, you can also start to add shares. It is still too small to buy shares in individual companies, but you can invest in:

→ exchange-traded funds (see section 5.11)

→ listed investment companies (see section 5.12).

You can follow this approach for several years, using Australian share ETFs, LICs or both. After about five years the $1 per day investment plan will probably be worth around $4000. At this point, you will probably have investments in one of the broad market index ETFs and/or three or four LICs, plus some cash collecting in the cash account.

If you feel comfortable with ETFs and LICs, you can continue with this approach for many years, or even forever.

7.3 Years 6 to 10—$3000 to $10 000

From years 6 to 10, we can keep increasing our investment in shares (through LICs and/or Australian share ETFs). We can keep adding to our existing investments, or we can add a further one or two investments to the portfolio for further diversification. But since the major EFTs and LICs are just keeping pace with the All Ordinaries Index and not trying to do anything fancy, it's probably not necessary to diversify beyond three or four investments.

At this point, the fund has grown to a size that allows us to begin adding international share ETFs (if the Australian dollar is at a high level), or property funds (if they can be bought for below their net asset value, or book value). This can be done by selecting one or two of the international ETFs that are diversified across several countries or regions of the world, or one of the property ETFs, which diversify across several property trusts.

We will also be starting to introduce the kids to the concept of money and how it works. We might be starting to give them pocket money or an allowance in return for doing chores around the house. We might also mention the idea of the $1 per day that we are putting away for their future.

Around year 8, the kids' funds will reach an important milestone. At this time we'll find that returns from the investments will start to exceed the amount of the contributions. The returns come in the form of capital growth of the investments, plus income from the investments (dividends from shares and distributions from trusts). Once the fund grows to $3000 or $4000, it will be generating annual returns of $400 or so (including capital gains and income), which is more than the $1 per day coming from contributions. This is a great achievement, and it will enable the kids to see the tremendous power of compounding and the value of reinvesting all earnings back into the fund. At the end of the year we can say to the kids, 'We put in $480 ($40 per month × 12 months, if you are contributing $40 by then), but the fund generated another $500 all by itself.'

7.4 Years 11 to 20—$10000 to $30000

During years 11 to 20, the kids' funds will begin to look like the type of fund that can generate the kind of returns needed to reach the $1 million target, as in most years the fund will be growing in value by much more than the amount of the contributions. They should start to look like table 7.1.

Table 7.1: the investment fund, years 11 to 20

Asset class	% of fund	From
Cash	5–10	• Salary deductions and child's contributions • Dividends and distributions from the investments
Shares	70–100	• Exchange-traded funds (Australian shares) • Listed investment companies • International share ETFs
Property	0–30	• Australian property ETFs • Listed property trusts

Once we have reached this mix of assets, we can just keep investing the cash contributions and reinvesting dividends and trust distributions into the LICs, ETFs and LPTs that we already have, or we could perhaps add a couple more every few years. This portfolio is in good shape and on its way to $1 million. The kids should be getting involved in the fund and putting some of their pocket money and money from other jobs into the fund. They can see that the more they put in, the faster it grows.

At this point there are a couple of extra options we might like to consider. They are by no means necessary, however, in order to reach the target. These options are:

→ direct shares (see section 5.13)

→ international shares (see section 5.14).

7.5 Years 21 to 30—$30 000 to $100 000

Our kids should take over management of their fund during years 21 to 30. We can continue to act as trustee if we believe there is a risk they will cash in the fund and blow it all on a car or travel and so on. But they have grown up with the ideas behind the fund for the past 10 or so years now, so they should be focused on the goal of reaching that $1 million.

When you decide that it's time for the kids to have complete control over the fund, the names of the accounts should be changed to remove your name. This should be done to the cash account, the online broker account and the CHESS account. The CHESS account can be changed by the online broker service. Ring the broker and they will send the appropriate forms. Once the CHESS account name has been changed, the CHESS service will notify you and your kids of the share registries of the companies and other securities in which the fund has investments.

By changing the names of the accounts, you are not transferring the assets in the fund from you as parents to the child. The child has always been the beneficiary of the assets in the fund, so nothing is being transferred and no capital gains tax needs to be paid. Of course, always check with your accountant first.

If the kids have a part-time or full-time job and a bank account, they should set up a direct debit from their account into their cash account. As they complete their education and enter the workforce or start a business, they will not see the regular contributions as a burden because they have been doing this for years. They should be used to it, and should have automatically built their saving and spending habits around their investment contributions, which are always taken care of first.

The kids could continue to invest in the same types of assets they already have. They could keep it simple and maintenance-free (by sticking to ETFs and LICs) while they concentrate on building their own lives, or they could get more involved in the fund if they want to by buying direct shares and more specialised ETFs. Figure 7.1 and table 7.2 show what the fund should look like over the various stages of the kids' lives.

Figure 7.1: basic building blocks

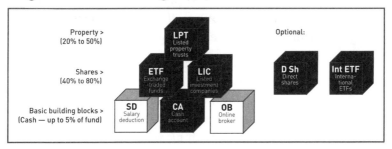

Table 7.2: the potential make-up of your child's investment fund

	Year 1	Years 2 to 5	Years 6 to 10	Years 11 to 20	Years 21 to 30	
Fund size	Below $500	Up to $3000	Up to $10 000	Up to $30 000	Up to $100 000	Percentage of total
Cash	Cash account					0% to 5%
Shares		Australian shares ETFs	International ETFs	Australian direct shares International ETFs		60% to 90%
Property			Property ETFs LPTs			0% to 30%

The proportions may vary from fund to fund depending on your preferences, objectives, financial situation and needs. Over many years of investing, you may become more comfortable with, or more interested in, a particular type of investment. Once the fund grows to a particular size, you can start to specialise in one or more areas if you wish.

7.6 Years 31 onward—the race to $1 million

After the fund reaches $100 000, which would be when the kids are around age 30 on the $1 per day plan, or much sooner if you make more contributions, the kids will be well on the way to reaching $1 million, as long as they follow the basic rules they have learned over the years of investing.

At this stage, the kids will probably be well into building their careers and having families of their own. Hopefully they chose their careers on the basis of doing something they loved doing, not something they felt they had to do because it offered better pay. What they choose to do for the rest of their lives should be something that they do for the challenge, excitement, fun, variety and sense of achievement it gives them, plus the satisfaction of making a contribution to society. No-one enjoys working just for the money. The kids' involvement in their $1 per day plan is designed to give them the confidence and freedom to be able to do whatever they want to do without having to worry about money.

Repaying the loan

The kids should repay the money that we put into the fund during the early years. Our contributions were always only a loan, not a gift. The repayment of our contributions (around $7500) will only put a tiny dent in the fund. By year 40, the fund should be worth around $300 000 to $350 000, and it will be generating returns of around $30 000 to $35 000 each year (including capital gains and income), so the repayment of the loan will not make much difference. They will still get to $1 million.

Keep up the $1 per day

Given the returns the fund should be generating by year 40, it wouldn't really matter much if the kids stopped making their regular contributions. But why stop? It was the habit that started the fund on the path to $1 million all those years ago, so they should just leave the salary deductions or direct debits in place. It is a good habit to keep. Instead of cancelling the salary deductions or direct debits, it would be a far better idea to increase the regular contributions. Or our kids might be having kids of their own, so they can start the plan off for them.

Time to cash it in?

Around this time, they may also be undertaking some of the things we did at that age — marriage, having kids, buying a house, taking on a mortgage and so on. It will be very tempting to use the $100 000 or so sitting in their investment fund as a deposit on a house, to pay off the mortgage or to buy that boat. If that's what they really want to do with it, ultimately it's their choice. It's their money, not ours. We just got them started and set them on the right track. They should have been putting in their own money since they were about 10 years old, and we will have stopped making regular contributions some years after that.

From years of investing together, we and the kids should both know that the fund is never to be spent. The plan has always been to build a fund that can generate investment income for the kids when they are 40 or 50 years old — to allow them to start a business, retire early, semi-retire, or take time off to travel or study, or just do whatever it is they really want to do. The aim is to live off the investment income and keep the capital intact. A $1 million fund can generate an investment income of around $50 000 per year and still keep on growing year after year, so the investment income increases each year. Keep the apple trees (capital) in place and just live off the apples (income). The trees will continue to grow and, as they grow, they will produce more and more apples each year.

Once the kids start withdrawing parts of the investment capital, this can easily become a habit. Before they know it the capital base will be eaten away and there goes the plan. It's called living beyond our means. We don't want to start cutting down the apple trees each year, because we will end up with fewer and fewer apples to live off.

What about paying off the mortgage?

There is a good argument that some of the money in the investment fund should be used to pay off the mortgage. Because we pay for mortgage interest out of after-tax dollars, it is better to put any spare cash into paying off the mortgage — unless we are getting an after-tax return on our investments of at least the interest rate on the mortgage. This is a very sound theory and I recommend it to anyone with a mortgage or any other personal debts.

Therefore, if the mortgage interest rate is 7 per cent, we should use any spare money to pay off the mortgage (or other personal debts) unless we are getting at least a 7 per cent after-tax return per year on our investments.

In our case we will probably be getting before-tax returns of around 10 per cent to 12 per cent on the investment fund. The after-tax returns are not going to be much less than this, and in the early years the after-tax returns will often be even higher than the before-tax returns. Why? Because most of the investment returns from the fund are going to be in the form of capital growth. Most of the investments are in growth assets, and we would generally not be selling these from year to year, or maybe never. So almost all of the growth in the fund would be tax-free (until the assets are sold, which may be never). And most of the income from the fund is in the form of franked dividends (which can generate tax refunds) and tax-deferred property trust distributions.

So in most cases the after-tax returns on the investment fund are likely to be significantly higher than the interest rate on the mortgage, but it is always still a good idea to pay off the mortgage (and any credit card debt and personal loans) as fast as possible. Should our kids dip into their investment fund to pay off the mortgage? They probably won't need to. They should have learned over the years to live within their means and to pay off all loans as fast as possible, so they may even be making extra payments on their mortgage without giving it a second thought.

Building wealth over the long term is still the priority. Houses come and go, mortgages come and go, but our kids may live to 100, so they need to be able to fund themselves throughout their life and also enjoy life. And we're only talking about a tiny $1 per day for the investment fund. After that is taken care of (by salary deduction or direct debit), then any spare cash should be used to pay off the mortgage and any other personal debts.

7.7 The risks involved in the plan

Going hand in hand with the concept of investment return is the concept of risk. Leaving our money on deposit in a licensed bank in Australia may be safe and secure, but its value will go backwards after tax and inflation and we will not build wealth in this way. Building wealth involves investing, and all investment involves risk.

Our simple $1 per day plan can provide wealth and financial security for our kids, but we also need to minimise unnecessary risks. So what are the main risks, and how do we minimise them?

→ *Loss of capital.* For cash accounts we only use accounts run by licensed banks in Australia.

→ *Broker fraud.* We only use stockbroker services that are owned and run by a licensed bank in Australia. In just about every financial crisis some stockbrokers fail, and the recent global financial crisis was no exception.

→ *Inflation.* We invest primarily in asssets that are expected to grow in real terms — that is, above the inflation rate. The plan also involves increasing contributions to stay ahead of inflation.

→ *Corporate bankruptcy.* Companies take risks and borrow money to fund their operations, and some fail — even large ones. When investing in shares, we diversify across a large number of companies in order to minimise the exposure to individual companies.

→ *Industry risk.* This is the risk that a particular industry or sector of the economy may perform poorly compared to other sectors. In our funds we diversify across all sectors by starting out with broad market ETFs and LICs. It is also a reason for diversifying into the international market, as this allows us to diversify into industries that aren't represented in the Australian stock market.

→ *Market risk.* This is the risk that returns and fund values will vary over time. The returns from all investment assets like shares vary from minute to minute, day to day, month to month and year to year. Over short periods like days or months, or even over a few years, share prices jump around, and so if we needed to withdraw the money in our fund on a certain date over the short term there would be no assurance that the balance would be anywhere near a particular amount by that date. But over long periods like several decades, returns from the broad sharemarket have been consistent. Since our kids are not going to be using the money for several decades, we are happy to accept the risk that the fund balance will vary up and down along its path towards the $1 million goal.

→ *Market collapses.* We recognise that investment markets collapse frequently, but we are careful not to buy investments when markets appear overpriced. In the case of international share ETFs, we don't invest when the Australian dollar is low, and we don't buy property funds when the prices are above their net asset value or when debt levels are too high. If necessary, we are happy to sit on the cash collecting in the cash account until we are confident that we are not paying too much for investments.

→ *Tax.* There is always a risk that tax rates will rise, and this would affect investment returns. While tax rates change from time to time, tax rates in Australia have been falling since the 1970s, and this trend is likely to continue in the future. Governments tend to go easy on taxes on investments in order to encourage people to invest, because investing creates jobs and reduces reliance on public pensions.

7.8 Market ups and downs

Our $1 per day plan is based on the idea that you contribute to the plan regularly, keep buying investments with the cash that builds up in the cash account, re-invest all the income from the investments, and never cash it in and spend the money. That's all very well and good, but what about market crashes, like we had in 2008? Do we just keep buying new investments, even though the markets are heading for a crash? Should we ever sell?

First of all, it is impossible to pick the perfect time to sell at the top of the market, and it is also impossible to pick the perfect time to buy back in again at the bottom. Our plan is based on investing primarily in Australian shares — supplemented by small proportions of international shares and commercial property for added diversification. Within each of these three areas we also diversify across many different companies (and across different countries in the case of international shares).

The Australian stock market has been one of the most successful in the world since it began more than a century ago, but it has its ups and downs. We saw in chapter 5 that the market goes backwards every three or four years, and then about every decade or so the market takes a significant dive, like it did in 2008. After each of these setbacks the market has recovered to get back on its upward path after one or two negative years. The last thing long-term investors should do is panic and sell out at the bottom, when fear is at its worst and everybody is warning that it's the end of the world.

The Australian stock market has generated tremendous returns over the past century because of some very favourable conditions we have enjoyed here in Australia: it has had the highest rate of population growth in the developed world, it has had high productivity growth, high levels of foreign investment, it is blessed with abundant natural resources that the rest of the world want, and it has strong legal, political and administrative systems. It has also helped that we have been a long way from wars, and that we have been on the winning side in the two major global wars. Most other countries have not been so lucky and their stock markets have suffered as a result.

These favourable conditions that Australia has enjoyed in the past are likely to continue into the 21st century, so we are happy that the core of our long-term portfolios are based on diversified holdings of Australian shares. To supplement our investments in Australian shares, we diversify into international shares and commercial property. International shares provide the potential to benefit from faster growing economies and greater productivity growth, as we discussed in chapter 5. Commercial property can often provide a useful hedge against high inflation, and benefits from our high population growth, limited supply and the fact that the population is concentrated in a small number of cities, as we discussed in chapter 6.

The problem is that all financial markets go through periods of booms and busts. While there are a variety of ways of measuring whether a particular market is too expensive, it is impossible to get the timing perfect to sell at the right time, then to buy back in right at the bottom. But what we can do is understand that there are ideal times when it might be better wait on the sidelines instead of buying.

In the case of international shares, we generally only buy when the Australian dollar is high (say above around 80 US cents), so when the Aussie dollar is low we generally buy Australian shares or property trusts instead (as we discussed in chapter 5). In the case of listed property trusts, we don't buy them when the levels of debt in the trusts get to excessive levels, or when values of the underlying properties become excessive (as we discussed in chapter 6).

In the case of Australian shares, there are also several indicators of when the market is getting to over-valued levels, when shares are expensive and vulnerable to a possible fall. At these times we don't buy more ETFs, LICs or direct shares in the Australian market. But what if all three market sectors are expensive at the same time, as they were in 2007 and 2008? When all markets are expensive, we are happy to buy nothing — just let the cash build up in the cash account while we wait for a better time to invest. There are times when cash is the best asset, as it was in 1994, when all other markets suffered losses.

Getting a feel for when it is time to wait is the first step, but getting a feel for actually selling investments is very difficult. One of the golden rules of investing is that when everybody else is buying (and urging you to buy) it is usually a sign that it is near the top of the market, and when everybody is selling (and urging you to sell) it is usually near the bottom. If you follow the crowd you are sure to do exactly the wrong thing. It takes years of practice to ignore, and in fact do the opposite of, what everyone is saying.

In my own case, it took years to learn how and when to buy, but it takes even longer to learn how and when to sell. Selling right is much more difficult than buying right.

If you do decide to sell some of the investments in the fund (as you may from time to time), always retain the cash in the cash account while waiting for a better time to buy in. If you take the cash out and spend it, it will be gone forever and it will be virtually impossible to ever get back on track later on.

One thing is for certain: if you make the commitment to start the plan and stick to it, you will have a much greater chance of building wealth for you and your children than if you don't start at all.

For more information about understanding more about markets and how they work, visit my website: <www.investing 101.com.au>.

$$$

We're investing primarily in shares because they are the basis of building wealth over the long term. The Australian stock market has survived world wars, depressions, recessions, market crashes, changes in governments, and social and economic changes for more than a century. We're using investments that are relatively simple, tax-effective, low-cost and diversified, and that have been around for ages and have stood the test of time. These are the ways we minimise the risks of this plan.

Chapter 8

Handing the plan over to the kids

When the kids are born (or shortly after you read this book!) the three main building blocks of their investment plan should be set up:

→ cash account

→ salary deductions (or direct debits) to put money regularly into the cash account

→ online broker account, linked to the cash account.

So while the kids are young, we invest $1 per day on their behalf. We will have been putting the cash to good use by investing in some growth assets. We have also probably been topping it up with the occasional Christmas or birthday present to help it grow faster. We have also been increasing the contributions each year to keep ahead of inflation. Now there's a few thousand dollars in the fund and it's rolling along nicely. The value of the investments goes up and down from time to time, but that shouldn't worry us because we're in this for the long term. It's time to start involving the kids in the plan.

8.1 When should we tell the kids?

It is much better to get them involved as soon as you can. The earlier they learn good financial habits, the better. It's a bit like kids learning any other habits. Just imagine if we didn't teach our kids to say 'please' and 'thank you' and to pick up their toys, clean their teeth and so on. If we had let them run amuck and then suddenly tried to teach them these things for the first time when they were 20 years old, we'd be fighting a losing battle.

If we teach the kids these things from a very early age, they become second nature. It's the same with learning good financial habits. The earlier they start to learn about spending, saving and investing, the sooner these things will become second nature. By the time most kids are nine or 10 they can do simple maths, buy things at the shop and check the change, and help with things like checking statements and doing some research.

Around about that age they can also begin to do chores and earn pocket money, so they are starting to appreciate the value of money. The $1 per day contributions will probably have grown into a fund worth $7000 or $8000, which is a serious investment to look after. It's also at about 10 years of age that kids start pestering parents for such 'vital necessities' as mobile phones.

Therefore, about the age of 10 is a good time to begin getting the kids involved in contributing to and managing their investments.

8.2 Introducing the $1 per day plan to the kids

It's best if you put aside an hour to introduce the process to your child. If you also have a younger child (aged seven or older), you could introduce it to both kids at the same time. Any younger than seven and it's probably better to start with the second child a few years later.

There's no need to cover everything in the first hour with the kids. You don't want to bore them to death. This session will just get the ball rolling. The aim is to spend some time with them regularly, telling them more about the whole process. Since statements will arrive in the mail monthly, this is a good trigger to spend time going though them and checking balances, transactions, contributions, income and so on.

Give the kids a box to put all their financial records in. It should be big enough to hold A4 folders and writing pads and sturdy enough to last several years. It is their special box, which no-one else should touch. The following items should go into the box:

→   an A4 writing pad — for notes and scribbles

→   a bound notebook — to keep records in (such as the cash account statements, shareholder holding statements, dividend and distribution statements and broker confirmation notices)

→   an A4 loose-leaf folder — for filing statements, transaction records and so on. Label the front of the folder 'The Junior Monty Smith Investment Trust' (or whatever the child's name is).

→   all the past statements from the accounts you have in the child's fund — cash account statements, share transactions, CHESS holding statements and so on.

(You might want to make copies of these for yourself first, just in case your child's copies get lost!)

→ a calculator—just a simple one with the basic functions will do, but it should have big buttons and a big screen

→ pencils, ruler and eraser

→ a copy of this book.

Wrap up the box with all the items in it and give it to them as a present, perhaps for Christmas or their birthday. When you give it to them, tell them that you will need to schedule an hour to go through it with them. And let them personalise the box as much as they want; it will give them a sense of ownership of the plan.

8.3 Lesson 1

Go through the following discussion points with your kids, using examples from your own experience.

Don't be like 99 per cent of the population—be part of the 1 per cent

Most people struggle financially all their lives. They work because they have to, not because they want to, in jobs they don't enjoy. Most have trouble making ends meet and some people have to work two or three jobs just to pay the bills. Only a very small percentage of people have enough money to do what they want to do, when they want to do it. Wealth comes from:

→ learning some basic rules

→ having a plan and setting some goals

→ sticking to the plan.

It's not about earning more money

Most people on a high income also have high spending habits and high debts. Also, earning a high income usually means working more hours, doing more training and being more stressed. (Several of my own colleagues and acquaintances have died young, through overwork and stress.)

It's not about luck

Many lottery winners end up with nothing after a very short time because they don't know how to manage money. Similarly, many people who inherit wealth often end up wasting it because no-one taught them how to manage their money.

Why kids don't learn this at school

Kids should obviously try to learn as much as they can at school and strive to get the marks that will allow them to get the kind of job they want when they leave school or university. However, getting a good job and having a high income doesn't automatically lead to wealth and happiness.

At this point, the kids will often ask, 'Are you rich?' or 'Are we rich?' Kids can come up with some really wild stories about who they think is rich. Generally, their ideas are based on what they see on television, which means they think being rich is having lots of flash things like expensive cars, boats and holidays. Tell them that being financially wealthy means earning enough from investments to enable you to do what you really want to do for the rest of your life. And that you are working on a plan for yourself and have been working on an investment plan for them.

The three things kids can do with money

There are three things kids can do with money. These are shown in figure 8.1.

Figure 8.1: the three things kids can do with money

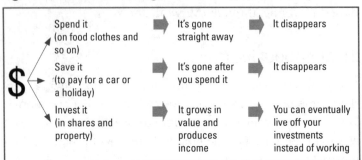

Why it's good to have investments

We might not be lucky enough to have a job we love doing. Sometimes we might not have a job at all. When this happens, we can fall back on our investments.

'Recessions' occur about every decade or so. During a period of recession, many people lose their jobs and many businesses fail. And we never know when we might be prevented from working—for example, through sickness, retrenchment, natural disasters and so on. So it's important that we're in control of our own futures and don't have to rely on others, or the government pension when we're old.

If we have investments, we can take time off to do things that don't generate income, such as travelling, starting a business or helping other people. And we can pass the investments on to our own kids or grandkids eventually.

Most people in the world have no investments at all. They generally spend all their money on living expenses and then borrow to spend even more. In the last few years we have seen several devastating natural disasters, including severe earthquakes, floods and volcano eruptions that destroyed whole cities and towns. There have also been man-made disasters — like the 'sub-prime' crisis, in which several million families in the US, Britain and Europe had their homes repossessed. Probably the vast majority of the people affected by these crises lost everything, had nothing to fall back on and had to start again from scratch. If anything like that happened to you, you would want to ensure that you had some investments to fall back on.

We are working on building our own investments and we now want to help start the kids off with their own plan.

Homework

Let the kids personalise their investments boxes. Ask them to look up 'recession' and 'global financial crisis' on the internet. As a reward for completing the homework, offer to contribute another small amount, such as $2 or $5, to their fund. The kids should put this money in their 'investing' moneybox (see Lesson 4, page 205).

8.4 Lesson 2

Make some time a week or so after lesson 1 to go through lesson 2 with the kids. Start by reviewing the previous lesson.

Taking control of your investment fund

It's time to introduce the concept of the plan and outline the three basic building blocks.

$1 per day since your birth

We have been putting aside $1 per day (or whatever you started with) into an investment fund since your birth. Tell them that your total contributions so far amount to $xxxx, and explain that through compounding of returns this amount has turned into $yyyy (put in your own numbers here). If the contributions continue at $1 per day and increase regularly under the plan, the fund will grow to $1 million by the time you are 50. The more you put in, the faster it will grow. And it's time for you to begin helping out with and looking after the fund.

The money we have contributed is not a gift. It's a loan, and you will need to repay it when you are older. By the time you need to repay the loan to us, the fund will be worth around $300 000 and you will be well on your way to $1 million.

Cash account

There is a cash management account with the xxxxxx Bank with around $xxxx in it:

BSB: xxx-xxx

account number: xxxxxxx.

The fund is in the name of 'XXX In Trust For XXX' because minors can't have investments in their own name. All of the assets and income are held in trust for you.

You will receive monthly statements showing transactions and balances. This is not a regular transaction account for everyday use; it's purely for long-term investments. There is no chequebook or ATM card, so you can't take money out. But there is a deposit book for putting extra money into the account.

Online broker account

There is a broker account with xxxxxx (an online stockbroker):

customer ID: xxxxxxx

password: xxxxxxxxx

account number: xxxxxxxxxxx.

You can use the online broker account to buy investments such as listed shares, listed property trusts, investment companies and other securities. Use the broker website to research investments. The broker account is linked to the xxxxxx Bank account, so when you buy and sell investments through the broker account, the money automatically transfers to and from xxxxxx Bank. Figure 8.2 shows the basic building blocks of the plan.

Figure 8.2: basic building blocks

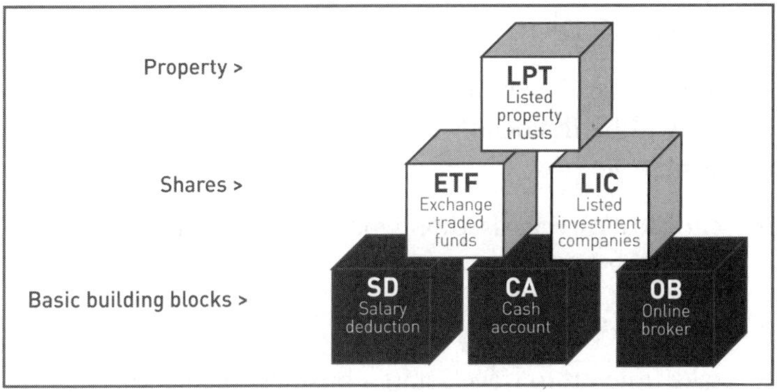

Rules of the fund

There are four rules in the $1 per day plan, and it's important to keep to them.

→   Put money in regularly.

→ Invest the money.

→ Reinvest all earnings.

→ Never take any money out.

What is the plan?

$1 per day + one hour per month = financial security for life

This is not the only way to build wealth and achieve financial security, but it's probably the easiest and most enjoyable way. You must start early, and you must stick to it!

8.5 Lesson 3

A week or so after lesson 2, spend some time going through lesson 3. Start by reviewing the previous lessons.

Outline the plan

The aim of the $1 per day plan is to create an investment fund so you will be financially secure later in your life. This fund will enable you to:

→ choose a career based on what you love doing, instead of what pays the most

→ survive financial setbacks

→ take time off to travel, start a business or spend time doing something that might not generate a great deal of income, or might generate no income at all.

We don't want to simply give you a bucket of money. You need to learn how to manage money and how to make it grow.

Introduce compounding

Go through chapter 4 (section 4.6), where it is explained how the contributions start at $1 and end up growing to $1 million. The $1 million in the investment fund can produce an investment income of around $50 000 per year later on in life, which is more than most people earn by working!

Most of the $1 million doesn't come from contributions. Most of the money has come from compounding. The amount multiplies all by itself if:

→   it is kept in the fund

→   it is invested in growth assets

→   it is never spent

→   all the income from the investment is reinvested

→   it is held for the long term.

Homework

Complete the exercises on compounding (and you can make up some problems for the kids to solve). You might also like to try the '1 cent per day for 31 days' exercise in chapter 4 (section 4.6) and see how far you get!

Offer the kids a reward (an additional contribution to their fund) if they complete the exercise and do the chart.

8.6 Lesson 4

Take some time a week or so after lesson 3 to go through lesson 4. Start by reviewing the previous lessons.

How to start

Whenever you receive any money—from doing chores, working, as a gift—you must allocate it to the following funds in the following manner:

Investment

Always put some money in the investment fund first. A minimum of $1 needs to be contributed every day.

Savings

Save up for large purchases—for example, you might save for three to six months to buy a bike or mobile phone; later you might save for one to two years to buy a car or to travel.

Spending

This is money for day-to-day items such as food and clothes. Most people do this in the reverse order—they spend first and then try to save anything left over, and then there's nothing left to invest. This is often why so many people have no investments, borrow too much and end up in debt.

How the plan affects pocket money

If the child receives regular pocket money of, say, $5 per week, they should decide how much of it to invest, how much to save and how much is left over to spend. Get them into the habit of deciding on the amount to invest first. Then the rest can be split into savings and spending money. A good way to start might be:

→ investing—$2 per week

→ saving—$1 per week

→ spending — $2 per week.

Don't make the decision for them. It's their money, so they need to make the decision. The only rule you should set is that the amount to be invested must be decided first. This arrangement can be changed later on, but we need to start somewhere.

How parents will help

Work out with the kids how much they will aim to contribute to the investments. Depending on the amount of pocket money the kids get, you may want to kick in some more to make it up to $1 per day.

Younger kids (who might get $5 or so per week) might agree to allocate $2 per week to the investments, so you will need to continue contributing the other $5 per week.

Older kids, who might already be earning money from work outside the home, such as paper delivery, mowing lawns and babysitting, might be able to invest the required $1 per day on their own.

Whatever option you choose, the end result is that the child agrees to aim for $1 per day and you agree to assist until they start earning a regular income.

Don't forget to tell them that your contribution is a loan that must be repaid when the child reaches, say, 40 years of age.

The three moneyboxes

Each child needs to set up three moneyboxes — one for investing, one for saving and one for spending. The kids should be given the task of finding and labelling their own moneyboxes. There should be a moneybox labelled:

→ 'investing' — to be kept in their investments box

→ 'saving' — to be kept in their investments box

→ 'spending' — this 'moneybox' can simply be their day-to-day wallet or purse.

Homework

The kids should finish making their three moneyboxes. As a reward you could contribute a $1 or $2 coin to their investment plan. Put it in their investments box until they make up their moneyboxes.

8.7 Lesson 5

Go through lesson 5 with your kids a week or so after lesson 4. Start by reviewing the previous lessons.

Making investment and savings calendars

Each time the kids put money away for investing, saving or spending, they need to do two things:

→ Put the money in the right moneybox.

→ Write down the amount they put in (for investment or savings) so they can keep track of the totals.

It's important that the kids record how much money they put away for investing and saving so that none goes missing or is accidentally spent on that great new toy they just had to buy. Banks and other financial institutions won't let customers deposit $1 every day, of course, so the kids will need to collect the money for investing and saving before depositing it. Figure 8.3 shows an investment calendar they can use for this purpose.

Each child should be responsible for keeping their own calendar up to date.

Figure 8.3: investment calendar

Investment Calendar

Year: 2011

Investments = Never to be Spent!
Will Generate Wealth for Life

Goal = $1 per day

January			February			March		
Day	$	Total	Day	$	Total	Day	$	Total
1	20	20	1	1	1			
						3	3	3
3	2	22	3	1	2			
						5	5	8
7	1	23	6	3	5	7	3	11
			7	1	6	8	1	12
9	2	25	8	2	8			
			10	1	9	10	5	17
12	2	27	13	4	13	14	12	29
15	5	32	16	2	15	17	3	32
			17	1	16			
19	3	35	20	2	18	20	2	34
22	3	38	23	1	19	22	3	37
			24	1	20	24	2	39
24	2	40	26	2	22	26	2	41
						27	1	42
27	3	43	28	3	25	29	3	45
						30	1	46

Running Total — Actual: $68

Running Total — Target: $60

$43	$114	$91
$31		

April	May	June	July	August	September	October	November	December
$121	$152	$182	$213	$244	$274	$305	$335	$366

Making annual investment and savings charts

Nothing beats a visual target to get people motivated to reach it. The kids can also draw up an investment chart and a savings chart for the year, either on paper or by using a spreadsheet like Excel. If they draw up the charts on the computer, make sure they print them out and put them on the wall next to the investment calendar and savings calendar.

On the investment chart, draw a 'target' line going from zero at the start of the year running up to $365 by the end of the year. On the savings chart, they can put the total they plan to save for the year. They can also write the name of the item they are saving for and draw a picture of it on the chart. This will give them a visual goal and remind them of what they are saving up for. An example of an investment chart is shown in figure 8.4.

As each month goes by, the kids can update the 'Actual' line on both charts with the amount of investments and savings they actually put away. Each child will draw up their own charts and be responsible for keeping them up to date.

Homework

Create the following:

→ investment calendar and chart for the next 12 months. The investment calendar and chart keep track of their contributions to the long-term $1 per day investment fund.

→ savings calendar and chart for the next 12 months. The savings calendar and chart keep track of their contributions toward a specific goal — such as buying a mobile phone, for example.

Figure 8.4: investment chart

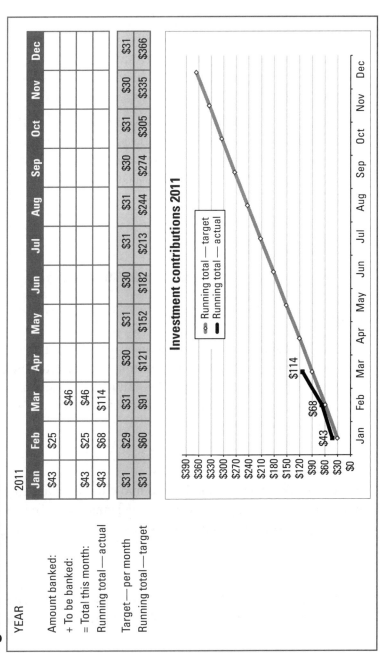

YEAR	Jan	Feb	Mar	Apr	May	Jun	Jul	Aug	Sep	Oct	Nov	Dec
2011												
Amount banked:	$43	$25										
+ To be banked:			$46									
= Total this month:	$43	$25	$46									
Running total — actual	$43	$68	$114									
Target — per month	$31	$29	$31	$30	$31	$30	$31	$31	$30	$31	$30	$31
Running total — target	$31	$60	$91	$121	$152	$182	$213	$244	$274	$305	$335	$366

Investment contributions 2011

Running total — target
Running total — actual

When the calendars and charts have been prepared, stick them on a wall in a place where the kids will see them every day, to remind them of the targets they are aiming for. For example, they could be put up on a wardrobe door, or on the wall of the kitchen or family room.

As a reward for completing the charts, you might like to offer to contribute $1 or $2. The kids can decide whether to put it into savings or investments, or a bit in each. The kids will need to record this on their investments calendar and/or savings calendar.

8.8 Lesson 6

Go through lesson 6 with the kids a week after lesson 5.

Inflation

Go back to chapter 4 and, with your kids, read the part about inflation (section 4.2). Use examples from your everyday life to illustrate the points as you go. You can make up examples and ask the kids to calculate the effect of inflation on the prices of everyday items.

Homework

As homework you could ask them to find old magazines and newspapers and compare the prices of items advertised in them to prices of similar items today.

Tax

Go through the section in Chapter 4 on tax (section 4.3). Use examples from your everyday life to illustrate the points as you go. Do the exercises in the chapter and set further exercises for the kids to do.

If the kids complete the inflation and tax exercises, they really do deserve a reward! Offer to contribute a $1 or $2 coin. They can choose which moneybox to put it into, and they should record it on the appropriate calendar.

8.9 Lesson 7

Make some time a week after lesson 6 to go through lesson 7 with your kids. In this lesson, you and the kids take a look at the investments that are already in the fund — the listed investment companies, exchange-traded funds and listed property trusts.

You should explain:

→   what the investments are

→   how they work

→   why you chose them.

It's a good idea to then take a look at:

→   dividends and distributions — go through some of the most recent dividends or distributions

→   statements and what the figures in them mean

→   the most recent annual report

→   company websites

→   the price performance since the investments were bought.

Homework

As homework you might like to ask them to read the annual report relating to one of the investments. (Annual reports are great for putting people of all ages to sleep!) They will probably have a number of questions that you may not be able to answer. That is a good opportunity for them to do some research on the internet.

8.10 Child's commitment and goals

After you have taken the kids through the basics of the investment plan and explained how it works, you will get a feel for whether the kids are ready to play an active role. Don't rush them into it — there is plenty of time. If you find that they are not interested or have trouble with some of the concepts, put off their involvement in the plan for six months or so.

When the kids are ready to start being involved and to take on responsibility, ask them whether they want to make a commitment to continue the plan. Commitments are always more powerful if they are written down in the person's own handwriting. Get the kids to make up a certificate like the one in figure 8.5, and when they've signed it put it in their investments box.

You can also set some goals with the kids, to keep them focused and on the right path. Ask them to read the part in chapter 2 on goal setting (section 2.9). They should each set their own goals with your help. Their goals might look like the ones set out in table 8.1 (page 216).

While the kids are starting to get involved in the plan, you will need to be contributing regular amounts to the cash account via salary deductions or direct debits. But the kids can start to put additional money aside for investing.

Figure 8.5: how to give your kids $1 million each!

HOW TO GIVE YOUR KIDS $1 MILLION EACH!

Ashley Ormond

My commitment

I, _____ , hereby make a commitment to invest $1 per day and one hour per month for the rest of my life in order to build wealth and financial security for the future.

(in child's handwriting)

_____

_____

_____

_____

_____

_____   _____
Signed   Date

Table 8.1: long-term and short-term goals

Long-term goals	Target date
• Build the fund to at least $1 million by investing at least $1 per day from today.	Child's 50th birthday
• Set aside at least $365 for long-term investment in the next 12 months.	One year from today
Short-term goals	**Target date**
• Set up three moneyboxes for investments, savings and spending.	End of this week
• Set aside $31 for investments.	One month from today
• Deposit $90 into cash account.	Ninety days from today

8.11 The kids' ongoing involvement

After you have had these sessions with the kids, they should be ready to start helping to manage the fund.

You're not likely to forget to keep the kids involved with their funds because you will receive regular reminders in the mail, and these are ideal opportunities for the kids to help out. These envelopes will all be addressed to your name 'in trust for' the child, so the kids will be on the lookout for mail addressed to them. This will include:

→ *Monthly cash account statement.* Check the balance and transactions.

→ *Statements from the share registries.* Check that they correctly reflect the investments that were bought or sold.

→ *CHESS holding statements.* These will record what investments the fund owns.

→ *Annual reports*, half-yearly reports and other reports from the companies and funds.

→ *Half-yearly or quarterly dividend and distribution statements.* Check that the money actually went into the cash account. If the dividends or distributions were reinvested in a dividend reinvestment plan, check that this is reflected in the CHESS holding statement.

In addition, you can get the kids involved in:

→ researching new investments

→ helping with transactions on the internet (but keep the trading password to yourself until you're sure they won't be persuaded by their friends to do some transactions just to prove that they can!)

→ helping to fill in the forms after you have made a new investment

→ collecting all the paperwork for the tax return or franking credit refund application at the end of each year — dividend and distribution statements, contract notes, cash account statements and so on

→ helping with the tax return or franking credit refund application.

Chapter 9

Where to find out more

9.1 Drowning in a sea of information

The providers of financial products and services are constantly changing their terms and conditions, and new products are being introduced all the time, so it pays to keep up-to-date and to find out what's available when you are ready to open accounts and begin investing. Here are some of the main sources of financial information.

→ *Online broker website.* You can use your online broker website to find out about shares, listed investment companies, listed property trusts and so on.

→ *Fund manager and ETF manager websites.* The large fund managers, property fund managers, index fund managers and so on all have websites that provide a lot of information about their investments.

→ *Company websites*. Most companies listed on the stock exchange have websites with an 'investors' section with information relevant to investors.

→ *Newspapers*. The finance section of newspapers, especially the weekend papers, is another good source of information about companies you're thinking of investing in, as well as such things as interest rate movements and inflation announcements. The best newspaper for long-term investors is the weekend edition of *The Australian Financial Review*, which usually provides a good wrap-up of the major news relating to the financial markets and investing.

→ *Magazines*. There are many magazines about finance and investing, with the *Australian Financial Review* providing the best coverage. Many of these magazines also have good articles that contain useful information and sensible ideas, but they are often lost among the advertisements and 'advertorials' (paid advertisements dressed up to look like unbiased editorial comment). By all means, read everything you can — just make sure you are aware of the biases.

→ *Television*. Most evening news services include a finance section, with reports on the All Ordinaries Index, the gold price and the movement of the Aussie dollar.

→ *Share tips over the back fence or at a barbecue*. Often when I am talking to people, they will say something like, 'XYZ is really going to take off so you better buy some shares in it!' But you should never buy or sell based on tips. Do your own research and base your decisions on your own financial situation, objectives and needs.

→ *The internet*. Stick to websites that provide factual information and are aimed at long-term investors — see section 9.3.

9.2 Useful books

The large bookstores in every major city have shelves full of books about personal finance and investing. There are books about budgeting, reducing spending, paying off the mortgage, property investment, shares, trading, options, futures and so on. There are many fine books on investing, but the following are 'essentials' that I refer to often:

Cottle, S, Murray, RF & Block, FE 1988, *Graham and Dodd's Security Analysis*, 5th edn (but any edition is good), McGraw-Hill, New York. Graham and Dodd is the 'bible' of share investing. Just about every stockbroker and fund manager in the world learns it inside out — or wishes they had.

Hagstrom, RG 1994, *The Warren Buffett Way*, John Wiley & Sons, New York. This is one of many books written about Warren Buffett, who is without doubt the world's most successful long-term share investor.

Lynch, P 2000, *One Up On Wall Street*, Simon & Schuster, New York.

Malkeil, BG 1999, *A Random Walk Down Wall Street*, W. W. Norton & Company, New York.

Roth, M 2011, *Top Stocks 2011*, Wrightbooks, Brisbane. This gives a good run-down of Australian stocks.

9.3 Information services

These services provide information on a range of products. Be aware that most of them are paid by fund managers and other product providers to provide information on their managed funds and other products, so be on the lookout for biases.

Investing101: <www.investing101.com.au> — This is my own website and receives no benefits or income from any product provider. Register for newsletters: <www.investing101.com.au>

Aegis Equity Research: <www.aegis.com.au> — research on equities, listed investment companies, exchange-traded funds

ASX: <www.asx.com.au> — good information on Australian shares

Australian Bureau of Statistics: <www.abs.gov.au> — the official government source of information on every aspect of the Australian economy

Canstar (formerly Cannex): <www.cannex.com.au> — consumer information on bank accounts, cash accounts, lending products

Choice: <www.choice.com.au> — good consumer information on a wide range of products and services, including bank accounts and online brokers

ETFmate: <www.etfmate.com.au> — contains comprehensive information, news and research on all of the ETFs listed in Australia

FundBroker: <www.fundbroker.com.au> — information on unlisted funds and trusts

Infochoice: <www.infochoice.com.au> — consumer information on bank accounts, cash accounts, credit cards, lending products, online brokers

Money Management: <www.moneymanagement.com.au> — useful news about the finance industry in Australia

Morningstar: <www.morningstar.com.au> — research on stocks, managed funds, exchange-traded funds

ninemsn Money: <www.money.ninemsn.com.au> — general financial news

Reserve Bank of Australia: <www.rba.gov.au>— the Reserve Bank of Australia is responsible for setting monetary policy (interest rates) in Australia in order to manage inflation and promote economic growth. Their website is a mine of useful information about the economy, interest rates, inflation, currencies, investment markets and many other related topics

Trading Room: <www.tradingroom.com.au>— good source of information on Australian shares

Yahoo Finance: <http://finance.yahoo.com>— information on and prices of every stock in every market in the world, including Australia

Glossary of terms

In the finance world, there is no getting away from acronyms. The following are some that you will come across in your investment journey.

ABS   Australian Bureau of Statistics — the main government service responsible for collecting facts and figures relating to all aspects of life in Australia <www.abs.gov.au>

AGM   annual general meeting — the meeting held by the owners (shareholders) of a company to elect directors, approve the accounts and attend to other matters

APRA   Australian Prudential Regulatory Authority — the government body that supervises and regulates banks, insurance companies and superannuation funds

A-REIT   Australian real estate investment trust — formerly known as a listed property trust

ASIC   Australian Securities & Investments Commission — the government department that supervises and regulates fund managers, financial planners and companies

ASX   Australian Securities Exchange — formerly known as the Australian Stock Exchange

ATO   Australian Tax Office <www.ato.gov.au>

AUD   Australian dollars

BSB   Bank-State-Branch number—the unique six-digit number that identifies the bank and branch in which your account is held

CAGR   compound annual growth rate

CFD   contract for difference—a derivative trading instrument that is based on the difference between the entry and exit price of a listed security. These are gambling products banned in some countries but legal in Australia (being the home of gambling)—many thousands of Australians have lost their life savings through CFD trading.

CGT   capital gains tax—the tax paid on the increase in value of an asset when you sell it

CHESS   Clearing House Electronic Subregister System—the computer that automatically processes the paperwork for transactions on the ASX. When you buy shares, you don't get a share certificate any more, you get a CHESS holding statement showing the shares you own.

CMA   cash management account

CMT   cash management trust

CPA   certified practising accountant—an industry accreditation for accountants

DRP   dividend (or distribution) reinvestment plan—many companies and investment trusts allow dividends or distributions to be taken as new shares or units in the investment, rather than as cash. These new shares or units are often issued at a discount to the current price and are usually free of brokerage and other transaction costs.

ETF   exchange-traded fund — an investment structure listed on a stock exchange that invests its money in shares or other investments

ETO   exchange-traded options — options that are traded on the ASX. Options are derivatives that give the owner the right to buy or sell shares in a company.

FSG   financial services guide — a document setting out information about the provider of a financial product that is given to investors by the provider concerned

GST   goods and services tax — a tax of 10 per cent on virtually all goods and services in Australia. You will pay 10 per cent GST on brokerage when you buy and sell shares and other securities. Most online brokers include GST in their brokerage rates.

IPO   initial public offering — when a company raises money from the public in order to be listed on a stock exchange

LIC   listed investment company — a company listed on the stock exchange that invests in other companies

LPT   listed property trust — an investment structure listed on the ASX that invests in properties. Also called a REIT or an A-REIT (see entries).

MER   management expense ratio — the annual management fee charged by managed funds, trusts and investment companies

NASDAQ National Association of Securities Dealers Automated Quotations Systems — the world's largest screen-based electronic stock market, based in the US

NYSE   New York Stock Exchange — the largest stock exchange in the US, and the largest in the world

PA   per annum (per year)

PDS   product disclosure statement—a document that sets out important information about a particular investment

ROE   return on equity—a measure of return on an investment, usually expressed as a rate per annum

RBA   Reserve Bank of Australia <www.rba.gov.au>

REIT   real estate investment trust, formerly known as listed property trust. Australian REITs are known as A-REITs.

S&P   Standard & Poor's—a large, US-based firm that provides information, research and rating services to the finance industry

SEATS   Stock Exchange Automatic Trading System—the computer system that carries out transactions on the ASX

SOA   statement of advice—a lengthy document provided by a financial planner setting out financial advice to the client

TFN   tax file number—a number needed to lodge tax returns in order to pay tax or receive tax refunds from the Tax Office

ULPT   unlisted property trust—an investment structure not listed on a stock exchange that invests its money in properties

USD   United States dollars

Index

Also by Ashley Ormond

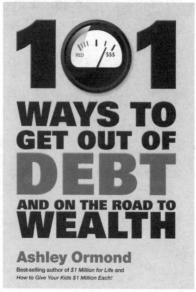